ALL ABOUT HEAVEN

Without exception, every human being faces the inevitability of death. Remarkably, very few ever properly prepare for it, nor understand what happens after it! My dear friend and co-worker David Oliver and his family recently faced the incredibly painful loss of a beloved son Joel. They had hope in Christ. They had an eternal perspective, but where is Joel and just what is he doing now? This exciting book answers, biblically, so many questions people have about their loved ones, their destination and their future. It's a must-read for us all, birthed out of deep mourning, ultimately to be experienced by all of us, and then the ensuing search for understanding. I highly recommend it.

Dave Richards, Salt and Light International Apostolic Team

David Oliver's story of painful loss has caused him to dig deeper into an understanding of heaven – both as an eternal reality and as a present 'home'. *All About Heaven* gives an excellent overview of how heaven is described in scripture. David recounts some inspiring personal testimonies from near death experiences, and gives us a clearer of view of what 'present heaven' is like. David brings clarity and insight to help us gain confidence in our eternal destiny. This is a very timely resource for all Christians.

Mark Mumford, Synergy Sphere

Many people understand that at the end of all things Christ returns, God will create a new heaven and a new earth where those who have trusted in Christ will live with him for ever.

But what about those who have 'passed on' well before this? Where are they now? What does heaven look like? What will occupy us there? When David Oliver faced the death of his son Joel, at the age of 38, following a short and brutal fight with cancer, he set about researching and writing this powerful book on heaven, committing to write whatever he discovered. This compelling and inspiring read looks at many biblical texts and provides us with a thrilling view of the future, a destiny well worth preparing for and looking forward to, which will enrich our vision and faith. I highly commend it, because I think we have seen all too little written on this subject, which is our glorious future!

Steve Thomas, Team Leader Salt and Light International

Perhaps one of the most difficult experiences in life to process is the death of a loved one. As believers, we are far from immune to the pain and grief involved. When the death is of a grown-up son who leaves behind his young family, well, the trauma is difficult to describe. In late 2018, David Oliver's son Joel was diagnosed with an extremely aggressive form of cancer and after only 17 days, his earthly life ended. As a published author, David found that one of the ways of processing this terrible loss was to research and write this book *All About Heaven*. You will find it to be an honest, raw account of what happened over this short space of time, but also the book grapples with our understanding of what happens to someone who dies as a believer. There is a lot of folklore and caricature among Christians about the nature and reality of heaven. David deals with much of the biblical material in trying to describe what he calls 'the present heaven', calling it a 'stopping off place' which is fantastic in itself, but also explaining that there is an ultimate destination ahead, when King Jesus ushers in a new heaven and a new earth.

All About Heaven will move you deeply but will also leave you scripturally informed about eternity and pastorally helped in the process of dealing with grief and loss. There are not many popular books available which deal with this reality; this one will be a great help to anyone who is unclear about how to walk through what is often a valley of deep darkness.

Gary Gibbs, Evangelist and Director of Elim Reach

The deepest question in life is 'What happens when I die?' and yet there are few books today that grapple with that issue. I am grateful for *All About Heaven*: it lifts my eyes, heart and mind to another world – more real than this one.

Rob Parsons, OBE, Founder & Chairman, Care for the Family

This book is tremendous and should be read by all Christians.

David Pawson, international Bible teacher

Many Christian books are written from the standpoint of theological study and original language research, which is, of course, commendable and very useful.

This book, *All About Heaven*, by David Oliver also has that aspect of being theologically sound and well researched but it is different in its origin. It was not born out of a desire only to explore for education's sake yet another important aspect of Christian doctrine, but was formed in the hot crucible of mourning, loss and sorrow. The result is that it relates directly to the common human condition, realistically and honestly answering questions that few have had the courage to address.

Having walked so recently through the distress of the untimely death of a beloved son, David has opened up his heart to us all and in so doing gives wonderful direction and encouragement to others who have walked or are walking the same difficult path.

Not only to them but to all of us who are yet to experience the inevitable death of a loved one, or our own death, it gives real and clear direction, hope and joy in the knowledge of what Jesus has prepared for those who believe.

David's book should be read by every Christian.

Peter Vandenberg, Executive Vice-President, Christ for all Nations International

Like so many of you, I have many friends and relatives who have 'gone on to heaven'. And while my belief in the eternity we will spend with God is solid, my understanding of what heaven is really like was weak. That is why I ordered multiple copies of David Oliver's book, *All About Heaven*. This is a powerful, useful, encouraging, and comforting resource both for those who experience grief and for those who minister to the ones who are impacted by the death of a loved one.

Rich Marshall, author of God@Work Vol. 1 and 2; and God@Rest. Host of God@Work on God TV

ALL ABOUT HEAVEN

DAVID OLIVER

malcolm down
PUBLISHING

First published 2019 by Malcolm Down Publishing Ltd.
www.malcolmdown.co.uk

British Library Cataloguing in Publication Data
A catalogue record for this book is available from the British Library.

ISBN 978-1-912863-24-2

Cover design by Esther Kotecha
Art directon by Sarah Grace

Printed in the UK

Dedication

This book is dedicated to my first-born son, to a best friend and co-labourer, Joel David Oliver. Extraordinary in life and extraordinary in death.

Thank You

I am deeply grateful for an outstanding family.

Joanna, I am grateful to God that he brought you and Joel together. I know you miss him most of all and I am so grateful for the selfless sacrificial love, care and attention you gave to Joel throughout your life together, but especially in his final months – you have been outstanding.

Daisy and Jacob, you have weathered your unwanted, brutal loss with dignity and strength. No dad ever loved his children more, and no children ever loved their dad as you have done.

Carleen, Joshua and Cheryl-Ann, you were beyond amazing in your proactive care of your brother and the family. No brother could have been cared for better or loved more.

Gill, my helpmeet and my best friend. You stood tall in the darkest hours, in the strongest winds, in the fiercest storms. No son could have had better.

With God's help, together we've made it so far.

Thank you

Preface

On 20 December 2018, the entire family and two friends were present for my son Joel's final hours. Just a few months earlier, he had been cutting down trees on our land. Now his body was but a shadow of its former strength. A number of medical staff stayed, because they had never experienced a death like it. There were blessings over Joel's children, prayers, and then as his father, I had the privilege of declaring the last scriptures. As the last scripture left my lips, his last breath left his. There was the last holding of his rapidly cooling hands, the last kisses for the one we had all loved. As I laid my head against his beard, still slightly warm, troubling questions were already forming.

Where did my son go? What is he doing? How did he get there?

Why is there so little written about present heaven, and why do so few Christians want to talk about it? And when they do, why don't they have much enthusiasm for the prospect of going there?

All these questions and many more rolled over and over in my mind, and I needed to find some answers.

Writing is not a new discipline to me. I have written more than fourteen books in the last forty years, but this book has been strangely different. I was apprehensive about what I would discover; nervous because, having just lost my best friend, somehow this had an emotional as well as an intellectual importance. Where is my son? The answer, inevitably, is so deeply important to me, so painfully important that I was afraid of what I might find out about his current location and his current activities. I have to admit, the early months of research felt a little like being on a rubber ring at the mercy of a fast-flowing current of anxiety.

I made a commitment to a friend to face this head on, and whatever the discoveries from the pages of scripture, I committed to write them. This book *All About Heaven* is the result.

Contents

Introduction

Imagination, Language and Understanding of Heaven

———•———

One of the great challenges regarding heaven is that while there is a good chunk of scripture devoted to the topic, it's full of imagery, mystery and allegory. I found myself reflecting on the research I had to do to get as far as I have been able in this book. Why has it been so hard to find a pragmatic, believable, accessible glimpse into what heaven is now? I have concluded that there are a number of reasons, not least, language and knowledge at the time of writing. If we include Jacob in Genesis, then the concepts of heaven are at least three millennia old; in Daniel and Ezekiel they are certainly two and a half millennia old; the writings of the Apostle John are just under two millennia old. What is clear is that those writers would not have had the understanding of the universe that we have now.

Let's take a minute to consider God's universe as you and I understand it now. We think we are sitting still as we read, and yet we are travelling at close to 1,000 miles per hour as the earth revolves on its axis once every 24 hours. Earth's spin, of course, is not the only motion we have in space. Our orbital speed around the sun is about 67,000 mph. As we sit here right now, the International Space Station travels in orbit around Earth at a speed of roughly 17,150 mph (that's about 5 miles per second!). This means that the Space Station orbits earth (and sees a sunrise) once every 92 minutes! Our senses and our spatial awareness have no concept of the fact that while doing nothing other than reading this text, we are spinning giddily around at 1,000 mph and then at the same time travelling at a staggering 67,000 mph in another dimension, with human beings above us in a man-made home hurtling around us at 5 miles per second. That is fact, it's real, it's every day – and yet we have no conscious awareness of it happening. We are both still and travelling at unbelievable speeds at the same time – an illuminating paradox that we experience every second of every day. It's a big universe.

What a big God and how big are his heavens!

And in this context, no one wants to restrict imagination as to the limitless possibilities of our learning and increasing reach through space. It's that imagination that fires sacrifice and fires the pursuit of knowledge.

You are probably ahead of me, but two applications help. Firstly, we tend to think that if we are sitting still, that is the reality that is real. But actually, sitting still in a chair is a perspective, it's not the whole picture by a long shot, nor is it the most important perspective. It's helpful to understand, maybe, but really, it's the bigger picture of 'the whole' that is the reference point of what reality looks like.

Secondly, no writer of scripture had any idea of these facts. Little wonder that in biblical accounts of creation there is no mention of these things. We do get enough in scripture to put value on imagination, vision, learning and discovery – and we do get to know that God created the heavens and the earth, and the sequence in which he did just that. We have populated our understanding with thousands of years of knowledge, sacrifice and learning. And yet who knows what our successors will know, see and understand in fifty years from now? And the point is, how could any revelation of this kind be articulated by the writers of scripture? Their writing was anointed of course, but filtered, informed, and to a degree limited by the known world and the limits of their imagination at the time of writing.

So through the centuries different thinkers, theologians and writers have seen heaven through the images of scripture and have attempted to apply that scripture to their increased understanding of the world. That knowledge has helped their perspective and increased their joy at what lies ahead.

What I have attempted to do in this book is take the ingredients we are given in scripture, and with the inevitable limit of 2019 knowledge and understanding, try to build an accessible account of what is likely, what is possible and what is fact. And in the process, I hope to unlock your own imagination and ensure you know you have permission within the bounds of scripture to imagine what present heaven is like. One thing's for certain, whatever you and I imagine, 'No eye has seen, no ear has heard, and no mind has imagined what God has prepared for those who love him.'[1] I have no doubt that Joel's eyes are now wide open in jaw-dropping wonder. My prayer is that you might at least catch a breathtaking glimpse.

CHAPTER 1

What Happens When We Die?

——|——

This question must be asked thousands of times every day. Every minute 105 people die; 6,500 every hour. By the time you have finished this chapter more than 1,000 people will have died.[1] How many times today will that question be asked? Yet how strange that it takes the moment or the threat of the moment for the question to come to the forefront. I think the Creator wants a change in perspective, this set of priorities, but it seems – particularly in the West – that our mindset is fixated on survival, on health, on staying alive, on a better quality of life – and yet how hollow all that sounds and feels when death stares us in the face in our family, when it's our friend, our spouse, or our relative.

Hebrews tells us, 'It is appointed for man to die once, and after that comes judgement.'[2] As we've just seen, there is more than one death every second. There is no doubt that every one of us will face death – it is even more certain than taxes. It is the one certain thing that every human being will face; every human being ever born has faced it. The only way out of life is death. One person in one dies. Old or young, millionaire or penniless, living in a mansion or homeless, alone or in the bosom of the family. One thing is sure, inevitable, certain and without any question – we will die. Unless Jesus returns, everyone reading these words right now will die, Christian and non-Christian alike.

Recently, Europe has celebrated the 75th anniversary of D-Day. Many stories get told over and over, as we give thanks for the sacrifice and the courage of the young men who fought to preserve our freedom. Those who fought would quite naturally have been apprehensive about the thought of battle, and if asked they may have responded that fighting in war increased their chance of dying. The reality, of course, is that fighting in the war has not increased their chance of dying. Every one of them would face death in the trenches or if they survived, they would face the same reality, decades later in their home country. Fighting in a war has not made death more likely, it has simply sharpened minds and brought the reality of death closer.

Given the 100 per cent certainty of death, isn't it surprising that we talk so little about it? We plan so little for it – the most important journey of all time. We live as if it is the most unlikely thing ever to happen.

Our society is on the run from death – we are not even supposed to use the word 'death'. With the death of Joel, I've watched and listened. People, even those with faith, are not certain what word to use. We say 'passed on', 'passed away', 'lost'. And when it does happen, we whisk the body away behind velvet curtains and cremate it, with a few canned songs played over an indifferent public address system. All that takes about fifteen minutes. What a strange, rushed and inadequate end to a whole lifetime! Even Christians talk little about it and prepare almost nothing for it! When was the last time you or I sang a hymn about death or heard a sermon about death?

This is not a satisfactory approach. Sooner or later we will have to stop denying death and face it ourselves, or with a close loved one. Every day 151,000 people die[3] and tomorrow you or I could be one of them.

For the Christian, death is different: it must be different, it has to be different, it really is different! Death is not a brick wall, it's not an unscalable rock face or a cul-de-sac at the end of life's road. It's a doorway to the greatest adventure of all time. It's the journey home after a long time away. It's a doorway to a new world, a better world, a world that we would choose now if we could. For those reading who are not yet followers of God, the truth is rather different. The choices made on earth are sealed at death, there is no second chance and no coming back!

When we go out on our family boat – even for a few days – there are hours of detailed preparation. We look at the weather, charts, navigation for day and night, tides, winds and full details on how to get into each new harbour or port. We work out who can go and what they can take. If research is to be believed, our family spends more time preparing for those things than most people ever spend thinking about death and what lies beyond it!

Woody Allen famously said, 'I'm not afraid of death; I just don't want to be there when it happens.' He also said, 'I don't want to achieve immortality through my work; I want to achieve immortality through not dying.'[4] Tongue-in-cheek maybe, but expressing something at the heart of every human being's deepest fears and deepest longings.

What if death was the beginning, not the end? What if the question was not about life after death, but this moment, this deep and painful distressing experience, helped us understand that where and how we live now is the shadow, not the reality; where and how we live now is pre-life and that real life, real living, real adventure is waiting for us closer than any of us had dared to think, hope or believe.

D.L. Moody, a famous theologian, said towards the end of his life, 'Some day you will read in the papers, "D.L. Moody of East Northfield is dead." Don't you believe a word of it! At that moment I shall be more alive than I am now.' A few hours before entering the 'Homeland', Moody caught a glimpse of the glory awaiting him. Waking from a sleep, he said:

'Earth recedes, heaven opens before me. If this is death, it is sweet! There is no valley here. God is calling me, and I must go.'

His son, who was standing by his bedside said, 'No, no, father, you are dreaming.'

'No,' said Mr. Moody, 'I am not dreaming: I have been within the gates: I have seen the children's faces.' A short time elapsed and then, following what seemed to the family to be the death struggle he spoke again: 'This is my triumph; this my coronation day! It is glorious!'[5]

At the moment of death, certai.n physical processes stop – breathing stops, the heart stops, circulation stops, though hair can carry on growing for a while! Then the process of decay comes. If man is only a body then, by definition, that must be the end.

But the Bible has another view. Ecclesiastes says, 'Dust returns to the ground it came from, and the spirit returns to God who gave it.'[6] Death is the moment of separation between body and spirit. Two things intimately entwined, which we have not seen separated before, becoming separated. When Jesus famously turned to the dying thief, his statement laid a clear foundation for us: *'Today you will be with me in Paradise'*.[7] The master was making it clear: the last breath here, the next breath somewhere else.

I remember times in Joel's extraordinarily happy and adventurous life when we really did lose family members: in shops, on vacations, in town centres. Interestingly, of all of us it was Joel who from an early age would keep watch. It was Joel who would ensure that the planning for our family day out included how to find one of his siblings if they got separated and, albeit temporarily, lost. I mention this because when we first talked as a family about how we would announce Joel's death, Gill, my wife, was very clear, and it was so important to her that we got this right. People said to us, 'Sorry that you have lost Joel.' Gill would say, 'No! He is not lost, we know where he is. We have placed him into the safe arms of Jesus.'

The imagery, the metaphor in her mind was important. In a similar way to the way the midwife had first handed newly born Joel into her arms, Gill was placing this same son into the safe arms of Jesus. We were certain he was not lost, and confident of his place, his location, his being in the next realm, the next life. People talk about someone having 'passed away' or 'gone'. The person who used to live here and live with us has gone but they have also arrived.

This is not just metaphor, it is a biblical certainty, and this thought gets expressed in prose, in poetry and in scripture in a number of different, helpful ways.

What is Dying?

I am standing on the seashore.
A ship sails to the morning breeze and starts for the ocean.
She is an object and I stand watching her
Till at last she fades from the horizon,
And someone at my side says, 'She is gone!'

Gone where?
Gone from my sight, that is all;
She is just as large in the masts, hull and spars as she was when I saw her,
The diminished size, and total loss of sight is in me, not in her;

And just at the moment when someone at my side says, 'She is gone',
There are others who are watching her coming,

And other voices take up a glad shout,
'There she comes!' – and that is dying.

Bishop Brent [8]

In this sense, it is helpful to think of dying as the loved one having gone from our sight but they have also arrived.

In the film *The Lord of the Rings: The Return of the King*, Pippin and Gandalf have a conversation about death not being the end:

Pippin: I didn't think it would end this way.
Gandalf: End? No, the journey doesn't end here. Death is just another path, one that we all must take. The grey rain-curtain of this world rolls back, and all turns to silver glass, and then you see it.
Pippin: What? Gandalf? See what?
Gandalf: White shores, and beyond, a far green country under a swift sunrise.
Pippin: Well, that isn't so bad.
Gandalf: No. No, it isn't.[9]

The Bible gives at least five metaphors to explain what happens at death.

A Shepherd's Tent or a Weaver's Loom

Isaiah tells us:

> I said, In the middle of my days
>   I must depart . . .
> My dwelling is plucked up and removed from me
>   like a shepherd's tent;
> like a weaver I have rolled up my life;
>   he cuts me off from the loom;[10]

It's a great metaphor from everyday life, originally written as a poem of thanksgiving by King Hezekiah, who was facing imminent death, as God grants him fifteen years more life. This body I inhabit is taken down and packed away like a camper's tent. Like a weaver, I've rolled up the beautifully woven fabric of my life as God cuts me free of the loom, and at day's end sweeps up the scraps and pieces. As a camper, my tent is a temporary dwelling, not my home. The weaver's fabric on the loom is never the end itself – the fabric is designed for another place and another function; it is meant to be set somewhere else doing something else

A Collapsing Tent

Our bodies are described by the apostle Paul as a tent in which we live. He says that 'the tent that is our earthly home is destroyed, we have a building from God, a house not made with hands, eternal in the heavens.'[11] Tents deteriorate with the ageing process of life, the weather and storms that they face, and when we die, the tent of our body dismantles or disintegrates. It's as if our body is just a suit of clothes worn by the real person. The Bible talks about the outward man decaying and the inner man getting stronger. As someone once remarked: a cemetery is no more than a cloakroom where we put aside the old clothes we have worn.

In Philippians and 2 Timothy, Paul enlarges the picture by suggesting all the delights of a long-delayed homecoming. This is the last of his letters, written when he sensed his time of death was close. He describes it beautifully as 'the time of my departure',[12] using a specific word meaning either time for me to 'strike camp' or to 'weigh anchor'. You'll recall his occupation as a tent maker, and his travelling, often by sea, on his missionary journeys. Either way, this established tent manufacturer, this seasoned ocean sailor, is using a picture drawn from his trade or a common but memorable moment from one of his many sailing trips.

A Departure

Paul talks of death possibly in the context of the sailing of a ship. In a familiar passage, he says, 'My desire is to depart and be with Christ'.[13] The word depart was used for ships that were weighing anchor and putting out to sea.

When we catch a plane, we go into the departure lounge until the plane takes off, taking us into a different dimension until we reach our final destination. Our bodies are like the departure lounge, left behind when we take off.

In either case, the meaning is the same. All the hassle, the lack of comforts and the deprivations of camping, and the homesickness most of us endure after an extended period in a foreign land are now past, with the joy of going home implicit.

Handley Moule, reflecting on 2 Timothy 4:6 said, 'That delightful moment when the friendly flood heaves beneath the freed keel, and the prow is set straight and finally towards the shore of *home*.'[14]

Falling Asleep

This description has caused some confusion over the years and it is important for us to understand it. The Bible uses the phrase 'fallen asleep' referring quite clearly to those who have died. Because of that, some believe that when we die, we stay in limbo – an unconscious state – until the return of Jesus. Some preachers have taught 'soul sleep'. In other words, when we die we enter a kind of spiritual coma, asleep in a non-physical body until we wake up to the sound of the last trumpet. There are many problems with this view, not least as it causes unnecessary distress to some, confusion or uncertainty to others, and can rob us of any desire to leave this earth. Interestingly, both Jesus and Paul used the term. Both of them in different ways made it clear that it referred to the body, not the spirit. In other words, it is the body that has gone to sleep until resurrection day.

I love the thought of drifting off when my head hits the pillow: sometimes just the look of the bed and the soft lighting appeals so strongly early in the evening I have to resist the urge to lie down there and then! I know some struggle with sleep, but for many of us we look forward to the moment of switching off and then switching back on ready to go for a new day, a new adventure when we wake up in the morning. As I write this, the family WhatsApp has a message from Cheryl-Ann who has just finished a late shift as a paramedic. There's a picture of her log burner in the background and the words, 'Yay for bed time'.

Falling asleep points us to the reality that death in the body is temporary, not permanent – we do wake up – and equally makes the point that we need be no more worried about death than we would be about falling asleep.

In Luke's gospel, Jesus tells the story of Lazarus and the rich man. Lazarus is in paradise, or by Abraham's side, and the rich man is in conscious torment, his spirit imprisoned.[15] Neither of these are in any way asleep. They are fully conscious and are talking, feeling, seeing and hearing. In the gospels, Elijah and Moses appear at the transfiguration with Jesus. Whatever else we might deduce, we can certainly see that they were very much alive, engaged and conscious. The strange story of Samuel being called up in the presence of the witch of Endor again shows that death is not synonymous with sleep.

Steven, in Acts, says: '"Behold, I see the heavens opened, and the Son of Man standing at the right hand of God" . . . As they were stoning Stephen, he called out, "Lord Jesus, receive my spirit" . . . And when he had said this, he fell asleep.'[16] It is virtually identical to the prayer that Jesus prayed on the cross to the Father and Jesus certainly did not sleep. Spirits don't sleep. This is clear from the story of Jairus daughter: 'Her spirit *returned* and she got up at once'.[17] It can't return if it was asleep. It was her body that was asleep and her body that stood up at the returning of her spirit.

In a number of ways, Paul makes it even clearer. He says, 'Therefore we are always confident and know that as long as we are at home in the body we are away from the Lord . . . We are confident, I say, and would prefer to be away from the body and at home with the Lord.'[18] In Philippians, Paul says, 'For to me, to live is Christ and to die is gain. If I am to go on living in the body, this will mean fruitful labour for me. Yet what shall I choose? I do not know! I am torn between the two: I desire to depart and be with Christ, which is better by far; but it is more necessary for you that I remain in the body.[19]

Summarizing this we can see:

- at home in the body we are away from the Lord
- away from the body and at home with the Lord
- to live is Christ and to die is gain
- I desire to depart and be with Christ, which is better by far

These four statements can only be made if Christians are immediately in the presence of the Lord.

Over the years, I have heard it expressed in different ways: death is a temporary cessation of bodily life, and death is a divine anaesthetic, as God performs an operation changing us from one body into another. In other words, death opens up a temporary state or an intermediate state before body and spirit at some future point come together again.

At death, the immaterial invisible part of man is released from its earthen vessel. In other words, we become disembodied. And after death, there is a complete and permanent separation between the spirits of the people who love God and follow him and those who don't.

The thought of death is not a welcoming or 'sunny' thought. In fact it is unwelcome; we don't want it to darken the door of our world, our family or our relationships. Scripture articulates a similar thought. Psalm 23 talks of the 'valley of deep darkness'. It's against the background of this darkness that the possibility of light beyond the grave is even more welcome.

Immediately in the Presence of the Lord

Falling asleep on earth, the believer awakens at once to the presence of Christ in a place called heaven. Paul is seen as always 'ready' to die knowing that to depart (*analuo*), to strike camp, to cast off and sail is to be with Christ.

At death, as the carpenter himself made clear, choices on earth determine locations at death. At death, Jesus told us, Lazarus and the rich man were conscious: one in heaven, one in hell; one in paradise, one in prison. They were both conscious at the moment of death and thereafter. Famously,

Jesus turned to the dying thief and said, 'Today you will be with me in paradise'.

Pauline scriptures we will read later remind us that 'absent from the body' is synonymous with being 'present with the Lord'. After death, the martyrs in Revelation are alive and fully conscious in heaven, crying out to God to bring justice on earth. In his trip to paradise those same martyrs seemed to impact John; they caught his attention along with other human beings there. And he describes them talking, moving, worshipping. All these references confirm we are not in a comatose state when we die. We are conscious, mobile, and engaged in heaven's activities.

CHAPTER 2

The Next Life: Reality or Fairy Tale

————•————

My son Joel was the most 'alive' person I have ever met. Far more alive than me, and I think I go some. 'Life to the full' took on a new level of calibration with Joel. I mention this here because with that backdrop, I was nervous that somehow what I might discover about heaven, or at least wherever he is now, would be dull and lacklustre in comparison to the life he lived here. And what I have come to see is that he is more alive than he has ever been – and I firmly believe that if he could choose, he wouldn't come back.

That's a bold statement isn't it, so let's hope we can find some substance to provide a context.

Few argue about the existence of heaven, but there are 2 common criticisms:

1. It is a harmless delusion – jokes about hell and heaven abound by the bucketload.
2. It's a dangerous distraction – an escapism to make one content with bad conditions.

The question 'Is there life after death?' is not new. Indeed, it is as old as humanity. And from the beginning of time, it has been answered with a 'yes'. Most, if not all, civilizations in human history have believed in some form of continued existence beyond the grave. Many people would feel that this is in itself a powerful argument for the reality of an afterlife.

Every culture ever discovered – to my knowledge – has had a concept of life after death. Whatever else different civilizations may disagree on, we all agree that death is not the end. I worked for many years with Ron Trudinger, a pioneer missionary who worked for a lengthy period with the Australian Aborigines, one of the oldest known tribes, complete with a belief in the afterlife. He and I travelled to Borneo and worked with the Punan tribe, one of the most primitive tribes on earth again with a belief in the afterlife.

Prehistoric man believed in the afterlife, as did the Greeks. The Egyptians went overboard with their elaborate preparations. I took time out to visit the Great Pyramid. One million stones each weighing two and a half tons, cut by human hand. The technology in their design and construction is a source of wonder. There is no mortar holding the stones together, I checked! Each stone – all one million – cut with precision and dependent on surface tension to hold the whole structure in place. I remember crawling right through into the final burial chamber. What a disappointment! Nothing there! It was a belief, but unfortunately an empty one, using the most advanced technology in the world at that time. Belief in the afterlife caused them to mummify the rich and famous.

I stood in the post-death operating theatre, where they used to perform some rather awful routines to get certain parts of the body out. Today it is cryogenics, preserving bodies in deep-freeze. Why? Because instinctively the human race knows that death cannot be the end.

The Romans believed in life after death. In fact, Geoffrey Parrinder says that it has become evident that no human group exists, however primitive, which has no belief at all in supernatural beings or entities.[1] The bulk of anthropological evidence suggests that every culture has some kind of sense of the eternal. This world cannot be all there is. Ecclesiastes reminds us that it is God himself who has put this sense of eternity into our hearts.[2]

Science has developed in this area. Near Death Experiences (NDEs) are now catalogued and researched. Cardiologist Fred Schoonmaker interviewed more than 2,300 survivors of life-threatening conditions, mostly in his own cardiovascular unit, and found that 60 per cent volunteered accounts of NDE.[3] One cardiologist, Maurice Rawlings, felt it necessary to embark on a serious study of the teachings of the major religions on the afterlife. This was his conclusion: 'I have discovered that the one book that is most descriptive of the after-death experiences of resuscitated patients is the Christian's Bible.'[4] We pick this thread up later in Chapter 7.

We can summarize these few thoughts by saying, some scientific research leans towards life after death. Most, if not all civilizations ever discovered have a belief in the afterlife. If evolution was really the sum total or even a part of our origins that would be extremely unlikely. In other words, the human race's propensity to believe in an afterlife points to a God who made us. This was one of Parrinder's points. It's God himself who deposited eternity into the very core of our beings. Surely that is a big, healthy confirmation that we should seek until we find what heaven is really like!

As we have seen then, this sense that we will live forever is not rare, it's not the exception, it's the norm in most civilizations. And yes, of course descriptions differ, but the dominant, unifying hope and expectation of the human heart throughout history is for life after death.

Seneca the Roman philosopher said, 'The day thou fearest as the last is the birthday of eternity.' A Greek named Aristides, in AD 125, wrote to a friend about Christianity: 'If any righteous man among the Christians passes from this world, they rejoice and offer thanks to God, and they escort his body with songs and thanksgiving as if he were setting out from one place to another nearby.'[5] And Cyprian of Carthage, in the third century, is quoted as saying, 'Let us greet the day which assigns each of us to his own home, which snatches us from this place and sets us free from the snares of the world, and restores us to paradise and the kingdom. Anyone who has been in foreign lands longs to return to his own native land . . . We regard paradise as our native land.'[6]

Some years ago, Gill and I made a memorable visit to Rome. There were many highlights, but the most impacting, lasting memories were from walking through the catacombs. Pagans, by and large, cremated their dead but early Christians buried their dead, and this subterranean maze outside Rome is testament to the tens of thousands of Christians buried, with firm faith and great belief in an outstanding afterlife. As I write this, I have a small Roman oil lamp replica, reminding me of that impacting visit. And as we shall see, the Bible makes it unequivocally clear that death is not the end.

As a family, we placed my 38-year-old son safe into the arms of Jesus. Okay-sounding on a superficial level, however the process of dying was terrible, brutal, distressing and deeply sad for his wife and children and our entire family, as together we nursed him 24/7 through the last seventeen days of his life.

In this unchosen process, Joel was magnificent: brave, selfless, taking care of the needs of others, recording audio tracks to help his friends and help his family. In his utter weakness, he still arranged all the practical things he could.

The point I'm underscoring is that his dying was not pleasant – it was tortuous for him. As a family, we experienced the deepest, darkest, most unimaginably shocking and heart-breaking, heart-rending, heart-stopping loss. So, you can understand that while each of us believed in the afterlife, each of us wanted that afterlife to somehow provide at least some measure of answer to the tear-stained questions. We somehow needed to know beyond doubt whether that afterlife would conform to our understanding of eternity in the heart.

Dying was no adventure. But having researched and written this book, I have no doubt whatsoever in my mind that as Joel drew his last laboured breath, he entered into the presence of Jesus and entered into the best adventure, in the best location, with the best experiences, making the best memories – all beyond the best and wildest possibilities that he could ever have imagined.

A Vague Hope at Best!

There is, then, a general willingness to believe in heaven but a sinister reluctance to dwell on detail. And I use the word sinister advisedly. Fairy stories touch the deepest human longing for something purer, better, in terms of both location and relationships: love, work and family in a better place. Think of any fairy story and the chance is it begins, 'Once upon a time' and it ends 'happily ever after'.

The human predisposition towards fairy stories hides a clue as to what lies buried so so deep. Instinctively, we just know there must be, has to be something better, somewhere better. Please God let it be!

Some of you reading this will have a view of heaven that's authentic, compelling, clear and deeply attractive. However, you are probably in the minority. There is, generally speaking, a real reluctance to engage fully in talking about heaven. Lots of Christians I have spoken to over the years struggle to talk with any enthusiasm about heaven, and the reasons we struggle are varied.

One of several dominant reasons is the fact that somehow heaven has been 'spiritualized'. It's apparently a spiritual place, with spiritual beings, and we're not sure we like that. We are not sure we can really relate to that. But if we took time to think about that, we would realize that it doesn't seem to align with Jesus, his lifestyle and his method of discipling. Artists, advertising agencies and others have fed us a picture of white-clothed angelic beings with benign expressions, strumming harps on a cloud. Misguided attempts to make heaven sound spiritual, i.e. nonphysical, distorts the truth and robs us of the ability to both relate to it and imagine it. If we can't imagine it, we can't define it and we can't look forward to it. Spiritual in this case is unhelpful – it leans towards the vague, the ethereal, and our minds find little to grasp on to or hope for.

Spiritual of course includes worship, and even though it probably shouldn't happen, we relate this to our current experience of church and church gatherings. For many Christians, based on our normal Sunday experience, our hearts do sink a little at the thought of an eternity filled with singing songs to our eternal God. If we are honest, we can't relate positively or with wholehearted anticipation of that possibility. But wait, hang on: if for many that is a real, heartfelt, authentic response, something is wrong. Surely it's not our apparently unspiritual reluctance to worship for eternity, but our view of heaven that is wrong – deeply wrong. It's as if we view earth as the best reality we have and heaven as something totally different, unattractively different. And because we feel a degree of guilt even thinking that way, we tend not to go there, and our thinking effectively shuts itself down.

Theological Confusion

It's not just our contemporary view of church gatherings either. Colleen McDannell and Bernard Lang state: 'While Christians still accept heaven as an article of their faith their vigor in defining the nature of eternal life has diminished . . . the desire to discuss the details of heavenly existence remains a low priority.'[7]

Many of the great theologians for one reason or another skip the detail of present heaven itself. In his book Randy Alcorn offers some maths, and I found myself provoked to do some sums of my own. Millard Erickson's *Christian Theology* has 1,272 pages. There are 7 pages on death and 11 pages on what he calls the intermediate state, but virtually all 11 pages deal with contentious doctrine – soul sleep and purgatory. Two of my friends have Wayne Grudem's *Systematic Theology*, which has 1,296 pages, and they have only found a single page on intermediate heaven. You begin to get the drift. Evaluating a small selection of commentaries, even where the subject is mentioned, there is virtually no detail on present heaven in 2,568 pages of contemporary commentaries and doctrine, around ten pages dealing, it seems, half-heartedly with present heaven. Almost no detail on our next destination!

When I studied distance learning courses with two Bible schools, there were lectures on the rapture, the great tribulation, hell, and the millennium, but I don't recall a single lecture on the present heaven. This surely raises a question or two: Does the Bible have very little to say on the topic? Why is it that I can't recall a single sermon in the past ten years being preached on heaven? Why is our thinking and conversation about heaven so vague or uncertain and, more importantly, uninspired? Why is it that in four decades I have never heard an evangelist preach on heaven? Surely, as a salesman I would choose to sell the very best benefits? Would Jesus focus primarily on heaven or hell? Surely, the former.

So we begin to see that the other main reason why people don't talk much about heaven is a relative theological drought, alongside noise and confusion in other areas.

1. The millennium

I have two friends who are world-class Bible teachers. One teaches that there is no future 1,000-year period with Christ ruling on earth. The other friend teaches categorically that there is a literal 1,000-year reign of Christ on earth. I can't gainsay either. I don't have the biblical literacy or theological experience. But I note with interest its impact on me. What it has done for decades is neuter my own convictions of eternal life and heaven. It has robbed me of the confidence to speak with power and with conviction and with authority. It's not the fault of either of my friends; it's down to me. But nonetheless, the effect is there. This book is my response. With God's help, I want to articulate with confidence to every reader exactly what happens when we die. It's one thing we can all agree on, and we need to be clear – life-changingly clear, hope-inspiringly clear.

2. Soul sleep

Some have taught soul sleep. In other words, when we die we enter a kind of spiritual coma, asleep in a nonphysical body until we wake up to the sound of the last trumpet. This notion often brings discouragement and even distress. It can rob us of any desire to leave this earth.

3. Two places called heaven at two different times

It's confusing that there are at least two places called heaven – one for now and one for later. That too is confusing – troubling even. There is what some call 'present heaven', an intermediate state which is apparently temporary and eternal 'heaven', the place of the final resurrection with a new earth, a new city and a new heaven. Because it's unclear on a whole host of levels, questions about the likely experience of Christians in both is also debilitating, putting a wet blanket on the possibility of hope-filled anticipation.

4. What about my relatives who have died before me?

What of those who I loved long before I became a Christian. What about my family member, my spouse, who simply doesn't follow Jesus? It can produce a torment of soul, looking ahead to an unclear heaven with an uncertain destiny for those I love. Talking to relatives and hundreds of Christians over the years, it's clear that facing the truth about heaven means facing the reality that quite possibly my loved ones who have died are not there. That is one of the harder consequences to face, and we address this just a little later on.

I was listening to the Gurung family speak recently. They were sent from a church in Stroud, Gloucestershire, UK as missionaries to Nepal. Since 2001, they have run a small education hostel for children of Nepalese mountain people. Their goal is to reach these young people, train them and then embed them back into the Nepalese communities after graduation. They shared the story of one Nepalese girl who was brought to the hostel, and who after some years developed an authentic faith in Jesus. Her parents, along with the whole village, were staunch Buddhists, and the unfolding story told of the deep pain and faith challenges this young girl went through, as first her father, then some years later her mother died. She was ostracized and marginalized by her own community. With her growing faith, she couldn't enter into all of the Buddhist funeral processes, and the resulting internal, theological and practical turmoil was huge. At times like these, belief in and understanding of heaven needs to be clear, rock solid and capable of providing courage, confidence and an all-encompassing trust in the King of heaven.

If the devil has one goal for Christians and heaven, what might that be? I think it's pretty evident. If he could get us doubting heaven, not even looking forward to heaven, worse still, slightly depressed at the anticipation of heaven, that's a demonic masterstroke of the highest calibre. Take out our hope, take out our motivation, take out our focus on the coming kingdom, and he's taken out our power on earth right now. I think that's clever.

I think if we could get a clear, compelling, inspiring view of heaven we would reach for it, talk about it, celebrate it, and the devil would bend the knee. I've observed pastorally, that the more people experience the death of close friends and family members, the more they talk about heaven and express their desire to be there. There is a degree of comfort in that focus, and the focus is often centred on the positive hope of being reunited. But even that, good as it is, is so much less than the All-Powerful Master intended our hearts and minds to see and believe.

CHAPTER 3

Are You Afraid of Heaven?

———•———

It's intriguing that so few Christians talk – really talk – about heaven. Ask yourself this question: When was the last time I heard a whole sermon on heaven? Strange isn't it? Those of you who have had any theological training, ask yourself how much did you learn, how much were you taught about heaven in your Bible colleges or online courses?

Science fiction writer Isaac Asimov writes, 'I don't believe in an afterlife, so I don't have to spend my whole life fearing hell or fearing heaven even more. For whatever the tortures of hell, I think the boredom of heaven would be even worse.'[1]

What on earth would give Asimov that fear? I think I may have a clue. We have explored a couple of thoughts in the previous chapter, but here I want to challenge one of the most popular notions, articulated in different ways in different church settings. That notion or inference is that one of the dominant themes in heaven is sung worship. Over the years, I have chatted to many hundreds, probably thousands of Christians about heaven, and most give it very little thought.

Those that have thought about it often view the topic of heaven as a depressing thought. For me personally, the thought of endless worship songs, and the absence of any sea could bring genuinely troubling thoughts. The idea that eternity could be an eternal sing-along, followed by yet another hymn is not motivating or inspiring. I appreciate that there are some who anticipate the prospect of unending sung worship with unalloyed delight. Well I'm glad for you, but please be aware you are likely in the minority.

Let me be clear here – the human spirit loves song. At a basic level, you can see that at soccer games, rugby, football, basketball and other sports. The sound of symphony orchestras, the quality of serious opera and the combined voices of mass choral presentations often leave us deeply impacted and inspired, with memorable moments. Music is God-given, God-breathed and when it's good, it really does us good. More importantly, it's one of the ways in which humans express to the full their authentic worship, adoration and homage. And there is an amazing diversity and breadth of Christ-centred, God-focused worship before the throne in heaven. The adjectives describing this in Revelation are almost breathtakingly grand, as they unpack the unthinkably marvellous new sounds, the levels of noise and the sheer scale of millions at one time engaged in authentic worship of a different magnitude, a different motivation and a different order. We see burning torches, flashes of lightning, the massed voices of millions in unison, described as 'like the roar of many waters and like the sound of mighty peals of thunder'. We read of 'a loud voice a voice like a trumpet the voice like the sound of harpists playing on their harps'. The point is, these descriptions are not more of the same old; it's not more of what we have just now. And this has to be faced personally and pastorally, prophetically and apostolically, and I believe it needs to be faced as a nettle that needs to be grasped now – for heaven's sake.

One of the challenges is that our view of heaven is coloured by our Sunday experience of ingredients purported to be a reflection of our expected experience in heaven. Right now, many charismatic Sunday gatherings are franchised reflections of big brands, commercially 'embalmed'. If I want to quote some lines from one of the songs in this book, I am likely to be asked for £250 +/-. I have visited some of the 'mothership' locations and watched on as music directors, through headsets, determine who says what, who sings what or who does what. The brand guidelines even suggest decibel levels and song lengths. I am not making a moral judgement here; we have benefitted as the church from a lot of good things deposited. I am, however, making a very practical observation, and I make it because I think the hidden impact, the unforeseen consequences impact our grasp and appetite for heaven. That, surely, is both worrying and serious.

Even in scripture, sung worship, while powerful and important, is limited. How many worship songs did Jesus sing with his disciples? How many worship songs do we find in the only New Testament blueprint for a biblical church gathering? The answer is one or two (see references at the back of the book for details[2]). Some might argue that I'm reading too much into Jesus' silence. I understand that point of view, but surely, anything really important to Jesus would have been spoken and recorded. I don't want to skim past this, because it is an issue and it seems particularly so for men. In his well-researched book *Why Men Hate Going to Church*, David Murrow makes the point over and over that what has come to be called 'contemporary worship' increasingly distances large numbers of men from a corporate walk with God's people. Take this short extract from Murrow's book, from the chapter 'I'm Afraid of Heaven':

> Popular notions of heaven strike fear in men's hearts. What man wants to spend eternity wearing a white robe, floating on clouds, plucking a harp? Men fear heaven because it sounds so dull. No challenge. No uncertainty. No fun. In heaven there's nothing to do . . .

> An eternity singing in the choir. Contrast this with Mormon heaven, where faithful men spend the afterlife making celestial babies. Or consider Muslim heaven, where martyrs enjoy the everlasting ministrations of seventy-two virgins. Guys, which sounds better to you: eternal singing or eternal sex? Is it any wonder why Mormonism and Islam are growing so rapidly and are so popular with males?[3]

Let me ask you this question: With all you know and have read about Jesus, can you honestly believe that he would want, expect and even purpose that our life in heaven would be based primarily around singing songs, however worshipful they will be? This is the Jesus who loved beach barbeques, worked with his hands, sailed boats, chose storms, went fishing, climbed mountains, appreciated the wonder of creation so much that the devil chose the created world to tempt him.[4] This is the Jesus who promised food and drink in the coming kingdom. The heaven many describe is not the heaven I can imagine Jesus describing, either then or now.

For Heaven's Sake

So it is that many of us find these thoughts of heaven depressing, or at least disappointing. Because so few of us have been exposed to any other narrative, we shut down, concluding that we are not spiritual enough. We lose heart and we lose desire, in what we know at another level should be the pinnacle of our faith, the setting we should long for most. And in losing heart, we focus on the tangible, the present, the enjoyable in this moment, and give ourselves to finding whatever life we can in the here and now, and heaven, even the thought of heaven, like a surplus railway carriage gets shunted into an obscure siding. And the evidence seems pretty compelling.

Among regular attenders of religious services 2 in 3 go because of their kids, and 1 in 5 don't usually feel God's presence.[5] Going to church shouldn't feel like a dreaded chore, but for more and more people it does. Type 'I hate going to church' into Google and you get 103 million results in one-third of a second. That means there are at least 103 million different articles, blog posts, and discussion threads online about how much people hate going to church. Type 'I hate church services' into Google, and you get 98 million results.[6]

Of course, on one level those statements prove nothing. Heaven is not flawed and what scripture says about heaven is not flawed. It's our view, based on our current opinions and experience that's flawed. I am making this point, not to swing the axe at church gatherings or church services. Let's pray for, ask for and seek some kind of change, renewal and increased authenticity. But I do equally want to face this head on with a healthy dose of realism. If one of the main reasons we don't love the thought of heaven, and if one of the main reasons we don't talk about heaven is because we are conditioned to believe it's merely a slightly better version of our current Sunday experience, that needs serious reflection.

And, like it or not, many are disengaged, in churches of all traditions. If the data is to be believed, many go to church gatherings because of obedience to the scripture 'not to forsake assembling', many go because of their kids and the experience is mixed at least. I was at a great charismatic church recently. More than 200 squeezed into a room. Great quality music led well from the front. I sat there with this chapter in mind and did my own impromptu research. No more than ten hands were raised in even the most worshipful of songs (that's less than 5 per cent engaged enough to elicit a physical response). In the last 6 rows (which I could see fully), during several of the songs not a single person was singing. There were 11 rows in front that I couldn't see. Assuming 100 per cent of those in the 11 rows were singing (big assumption), that is still a staggering 35 per cent apparently disengaged. I was at another church a few weeks later. In the two most worshipful songs, less than half the congregation were singing at the same time and fewer than 10 were raising their hands.

Yes, I know there are all kinds of caveats, but I have travelled enough and preached enough to know that in the West these are not unusual observations. The numbers vary a bit from church to church and from meeting to meeting but the trend is there. If you're a church leader in the West, you are already facing church membership where large numbers will never attend every service in a month. And if you would ask your congregation individually and in a 'safe setting' whether they long to go to church next Sunday . . . I think you already know what the answer is likely to be.

Again, there are all kinds of caveats, but bear in mind this represents the views and beliefs and experience of those who still come along. The UK trajectory, including some new churches, has seen a steady decline. Overall in the UK, church attendance has gone from 5 million in 1980 to 2.45 million in 2015.[7]

The point of sharing this data is simple but rather important. If heaven is perceived as a turbocharged endless worship service or an eternal church meeting sing-along, similar in some way to our experience of contemporary church gatherings, then many of God's people struggle with that thought. It is so disappointing and leaves the individual with a slightly guilty feeling: *I know if I was godly I should long for this but . . .*

We should gasp at thoughts of heaven like a drowning man whose head surfaces above the downward pull. Our lives on earth should be resonating with purpose at the thought of what is to come. Our choices on earth should be deeply impacted, like a wise investment based on a heavenly return. Our minds should be filled with wonder at the possibilities that await us, not secretly dreading the very thought. And yet many of God's people it seems, because of false notions and the ensuing disappointment and accompanying feelings of guilt, keep silent and don't even go there in thinking, conversations or anticipation.

Longing to Go Home

Contrast this apparent reluctance to engage in thoughts of heaven with what the writers of scripture have to say: 'Beloved, I urge you as sojourners and exiles to abstain from the passions of the flesh, which wage war against your soul.'[8]

Being an exile is being resident, but as a foreigner, and in Hebrews this concept is expressed even more clearly. Talking about Abraham and other heroes of the faith the writer says: 'These all died in faith . . . they were strangers and exiles on the earth . . . they desire a better country, that is, a heavenly one. Therefore God is not ashamed to be called their God, for he has prepared for them a city.[9]

The truth is we are residents on earth and in our culture, but we are really aliens, we don't belong here. Peter says that we are 'born again to a living hope . . . to an inheritance that is imperishable, undefiled and unfading, kept in heaven for you. In this you rejoice, though now for a little while, if necessary, you have been grieved by various trials'.[10]

Paul reminds us that 'while we are in at home in the body we are away from the Lord'.[11] God has put eternity in our hearts. Eternity is our home; this green and blue planet, beautiful as it is, is not our true home. These scriptures remind us that the compass bearing of our hopes, our deepest longings and beliefs swing always to true north – to be with the Lord. It is the heart's magnetic pull, inexorably pointing to heaven.

One of the songs from the Christian music scene in my twenties, has never left me: 'Going' home I am always going home inside; there's an ache in my heart that I can't bear'.[12] That song touches something deep in me.

When I was 21 years old, my mother and I nursed my father through cancer, and I will never forget the final moments. We had fasted, prayed, had the best medical input and we had fought for his life. But at the moment of his death, in a setting full of the presence of God, I found myself singing spontaneously a song popular at the time: 'Your loving kindness is better than life, my lips will praise you'. It was a moment of praise in sorrow and a moment of profound revelation when I saw it from God's perspective. The human desire is to prevent death and to hold onto life here. But at that moment I 'saw' that to be with Christ is far better than life, and something changed at a very deep level in me that day.

I can't wait for my next home. I believe in eternal life, I believe that heaven is better by far, and I believe that for me to live is

Christ and to die is gain, to die is better. To die is the doorway to an even better life and I can't wait. I love the life I have here. I love Gill, my family, my home, my work, but I know the next life is exponentially better. And if I really do believe that, it makes handling suffering, persecution and misunderstanding easier in the here and now.

When Gill and I were first married, she was fearful of death. When I asked why it became apparent that it was because she thought being married was so wonderful she didn't want to lose it in heaven. She doesn't feel that quite so strongly these days! But actually, it was an important issue for us to talk through and walk through over time.

Here's a question I heard David Pawson pose that can be quite revealing, even a bit disturbing, and how you and I answer it in our heart is also quite revealing:

Are you willing to stay but longing to go?
    or
Are you longing to stay and willing to go?

The answer to that question is important because it reveals to each of us what's most important – this life or the next. And that reality affects how we live now and how we handle living for God with full abandon now.

What a contrast from Charles Spurgeon: 'To come to thee is to come home from exile, to come to land out of the raging storm, to come to rest after long labour, to come to the goal of my desires and the summit of my wishes.'[13]

Jonathan Edwards the great Puritan preacher often spoke about heaven. He said, 'It becomes us to spend this life only as a journey toward heaven . . . to which we should subordinate all other concerns of life. Why should we labor for or set our hearts on anything else, but that which is our proper end and true happiness?'[14] G.K. Chesterton wrote, 'The modern philosopher had told me again and again that I was in the right place, and I had still felt depressed even in acquiescence . . . When I heard that I was in the wrong place. . . my soul sang for joy, like a bird in spring. I knew now . . . why I could feel homesick at home.'[15] C.S. Lewis said, 'If I find in myself a desire which no experience in this world can satisfy, the most probable explanation is that I was made for another world.'[16]

When I travel as I often do, and have done all my life, if I'm away for any length of time I get desperate for home. I ache for the familiar: Gill, the kids and story time, my log fire and the logs my hands have chopped, my own bed with the wonderful view from my window, and the patchwork quilt on my bed made with skill and love in over 1,000 hours of labour. This is real, and you and I can identify with it I'm sure, but even then, I am not fully at rest. I love the way the writer to the Hebrews (talking about some of the heroes of the faith) describes it: they were strangers and exiles seeking a homeland, looking for a place to call home. He says that they did not receive the things they had been promised – they only saw them and welcomed them from a distance, admitting that they were foreigners and strangers on earth. People who say such things show that they are looking for a country of their own. For here we do not have an enduring city, but we are looking for the city that is to come, that God has prepared for us.[17]

Jesus himself had this same deep longing for home. In John 14 he says to the disciples, 'I am going away . . . If you loved me, you would have rejoiced, because I am going to the Father. And in John 17 he says, 'I am coming to you. Holy Father, keep them in your name'. He goes on to say that he longs for his disciples to be with him in that place, 'Father, I desire that they also, whom you have given me, may be with me where I am.'[18]

I'm a sailor and one of the items you to learn to respect early on is the compass. Wherever you are in the world, whatever the conditions, whether it's night or day that compass will tell you, remind you, point you to magnetic north. Every navigational decision, large or small, is made on the basis of that irrefutable fact. And only a fool doesn't believe it or heed it. Heaven is my magnetic pull, it's where I long to be and my heart will not be fully at rest until I'm there. It really is true, 'I am always goin' home inside; there's an ache in my heart that I can't hide'. That song is like an anthem reflecting the desires of my heart and it's never waned.

I'm also a rugby fan, my sons Joel and Joshua loved nothing better than for us to be cheering the England team on for 6 nations or World Cup at Twickenham. We were always mischievous and would love to start the stadium anthem which would then be picked up by tens of thousands of supporters and roll its' loudly magnificent way, all-round the stadium. The anthem is an old African American spiritual song, 'Swing low, sweet chariot, coming for to carry me home'. The same genre of songs produced the well-known song that Jim Reeves made famous, 'This world is not my home'.[19] The African American Spiritual genre owes its existence to a number of factors, but one undergirding reality was that in the distress of the present, the suffering slaves could best handle the present suffering by reminding themselves of the true home of heaven which awaited.

The best articulation of this longing that I have heard is by Randy Alcorn in his book *Heaven*. He says: 'I've never been to heaven, yet I miss it. Eden's in my blood. The best things of life are souvenirs from Eden, appetizers of the new earth. There are just enough of them to keep us going, but never enough to make us satisfied with the world as it is, or ourselves as we are.' [20]

CHAPTER 4

Heaven: A Popular View

———·———

Here's an interesting question to ponder. When you read or hear the word 'heaven' what immediately comes to your mind? I wonder what you 'saw' in your mind's eye. Chances are that what you 'saw' in some way reflects the beliefs you hold that influence and shape your view of heaven.

It's an interesting word because society has come to use heaven in a frivolous way to define anything extremely pleasurable from holidays to chocolate to ice cream. What's interesting on a more thoughtful plane is that most of us view heaven as a place we go to when we die. The Bible includes that but has a distinct focus on heaven as the place where God dwells *now*. Time and again in scripture, heaven and earth appear to be connected, and what goes on in heaven is believed to be significantly connected to what happens on earth now.

It's interesting too that we have a man-centred approach to heaven, whether or not that's the popular use of it, to describe a beautiful experience or to describe a place of rest and peace that we hope our loved ones enjoy after death. It will often feature in art and music, profoundly so with Eric Clapton's 'Tears in Heaven' in which he asks his 4-year-old son if he would know his name if he saw him in heaven.[1] Later in this book I think we can answer that question. Bob Dylan talked about 'knocking on heaven's door' and more recently, Steven Curtis Chapman in an altogether more positive album talks about the 'glorious unfolding'.

Whatever the merits of these songs, popular attitudes to heaven are somewhat vague and ambiguous, and do seem to revolve around where we go when we die and what happens when we get there. If I reflect honestly on my reason for researching and writing this book, I have to admit this was a driver. I wanted to know where Joel had gone and understand what he is doing there. That's a very simple, limited and self-referential view of heaven with a focus on Joel the person who has left us. On one level, this is quite understandable. Most of what I have thought and believed has come from funerals, committals and thanksgiving services. In nearly every case, the primary focus at these events is personal and individual. The tributes and eulogies are primarily about the loved ones who have left us, again reinforcing this self-referential view of heaven. It's equally understandable that people suffering from a terminal or incurable sickness often have an insatiable curiosity about the afterlife, and heaven in particular.

The Bible, however, seems much more concerned about heaven as the place where God is now, and the compelling suggestion that heaven is integrally related to our world. Over and over the biblical texts seem to shout at us that heaven is the place where God dwells above the earth and from which God intervenes in the affairs of earth, and in particular his kingdom. It's not primarily about the individual destination after this life.

Finding a clear definition of the word 'heaven' poses a challenge. It's a flexible word: heaven is used both in popular language and in scripture to refer to clouds and blue sky. In English translations of the Bible, commonly, when the Hebrew word refers to the sky the plural 'heavens' is used and when it's meaning is God's dwelling place the singular 'heaven' is used.

Take a look at the three scriptures below:

I will give thanks to you, O Lord, among the peoples;
I will sing praises to you among the nations.
For your steadfast love is great to the heavens,
your faithfulness to the clouds.
Be exalted, O God, above the heavens!
Let your glory be over all the earth![2]

I cry out to God Most High,
to God who fulfils his purpose for me.
He will send from heaven and save me;[3]

Behold, to the LORD your God belong heaven and the heaven of heavens,[4]

This appears at first glance a little confusing, but actually, like a clue on a treasure hunt it opens up information that is essential to finding the treasure. In Genesis we are told,

'God created the heavens and the earth'[5] and from the very first descriptions available we get this sense of the sky (and probably the atmosphere) together with the invisible but close by location of God. And we get the earliest of clues that heaven and earth in God's mind, in God's purpose and in God's heart are close, and are part of one created effort. It seems that the Bible views heaven, the heavens and the earth as one integrated world or one universe. In approximately one quarter of the scriptures on heaven – over 100 times – both heaven and earth appear together in the same verse. It's clear then that scripture has a view of heaven that is way beyond the individual, the privatized, the personal.

Heaven and Earth Connected

In Genesis, the relationship between heaven and earth was so close it seems God could take a stroll from one to the other. It's fitting that it's the first few pages of our Bible and the last few pages of our Bible that make this past and future connection clear. The first pages of scripture talk about a God who would walk with his creation on earth. God's desire, his design, his intent has always been to live with us. The fall destroyed that design and God and man were separated on earth and in heaven.

And yet, while at the fall heaven withdrew, it may not be as far away as we think. In Genesis, cherubim are placed with 'a flaming sword that turned every way to guard the way to the tree of life'.[6] This very tree, Revelation informs us, is right now in present heaven. This sounds like the stuff of science fiction. The reality then is that heaven is closer than we think and yet in terms of accessibility further away than we want. The biblical tradition suggests that heaven was created alongside earth and may well be hidden from us currently, but actually all the evidence suggests that it is likely quite close. I've heard it suggested from a variety of sources and with some scientific rationale that it may be in a parallel universe. I have no idea whether that is true or not, but I understand the logic.

To reiterate the point: from the beginning of time, God created heaven and earth together. They continue to co-exist, and Revelation makes it clear that they will be remade into a new heaven and a new earth. From the very first pages to the very last pages of our Bibles we see God's intent: these realms are part of one universe – they are connected and meant to be interrelated.

This connectedness between heaven and earth appears in a number of places in the Bible. In Genesis, Jacob has a dream in which there was a ladder with angels ascending and descending, and Jacob tells us he was at the 'gate of heaven'.[7]

Peter tells us that the Holy Spirit is sent from heaven.[8] Steven, at the moment of his death in a short but real Near-Death Experience (NDE), sees heaven open and gazes on the glory of God and Jesus standing at the right hand of God.[9] Three of the gospels talk about heaven being opened at the baptism of Jesus. Just as Steven could look up into heaven, it seems in the gospels that God was looking down visibly and speaking audibly to earth. In the narrative around the birth of Jesus we see a heavenly host appear!

Key to the apostle Paul's conversion experience was the light around him. In the book of Acts, it seems like the story unfolds with a little more clarity at each iteration. In the first instance, he hears a voice from heaven. By the time the story is being retold in Acts 22 it's described as 'a great light from heaven' and in the final iteration in Acts 26 it becomes described as a 'light from heaven; brighter than the sun.' Somehow, to Paul this was extremely significant.[10]

The apostle John is called into present heaven in the book of Revelation and seems to see the new heaven and new earth from his vantage point of the present. Three times in three places he is told to write, 'Blessed are those who die in the Lord from now on.'[11] It's another solid encouragement to believe that when we die we are immediately in the presence of the Lord and it's better than anything we have experienced to date and better than anything we could imagine.

One of the big changes between Old and New Testament perspectives is the gateway: for Jacob it was a place where he saw angels ascending and descending, but now it is a person – Jesus. Jesus proclaims to Nathanael that he will get to see 'angels ascending and descending on the Son of Man'.[12] It's interesting to note that the point of these experiences for Bible characters such as Jacob, Stephen, Paul and John, as well as others like Daniel and Ezekiel, was not the experience of heaven itself but rather the link, the dawning realization that what they had experienced of heaven in their various experiences was somehow inextricably linked with the purposes of God on earth.

This connectedness appears overtly in the theology of some Christian traditions. I had the joy and adventure recently of visiting some friends who live near Paphos in Cyprus. There is a strong traditional Greek Orthodox presence on the island and one of the memorable adventures we enjoyed was visiting a painted cave in a rural area called Kouklia. In a strange procedure, you simply call at a small tourist office close to the local church, collect a key and you are free to visit the cave on your own. A trek in a 4x4 and a bit of a walk takes you to a hollowed-out cave dating back to the fifteenth century. The cave had been inhabited by a godly hermit and the ceiling and some of the walls are covered with exquisite paintings. While the paintings have been defaced (probably by Muslim shepherds over the years), it is still possible to see in this beautifully and meticulously adorned hemisphere, a reflection of the theology of the occupant. What the art depicts is earth, heaven and the heaven of heavens all connected, essentially in a vaulted universe. Father Son and Sprit are depicted next to archangels, angels, seraphim, cherubim and the wheels of Ezekiel, connected in turn to the gospel writers and scenes on earth. The detail requires an expert to fully appreciate, but the overall impact is unmistakable. This was painted by a person or for a person who believed in a totally connected universe of earth, the heavens and the heaven of heavens.

In 1961 Yuri Gagarin was the first human to enter space. He is reputed to have said, 'I looked and looked but didn't see God.'

Many were quick to interpret this as a statement of atheistic denial in God. Not so. Gagarin was a Russian Orthodox and would have been taught to live with the notion that heaven was somewhere above the atmosphere. It may be that his theology needed some small recalibration in terms of latitude and longitude but his expectation, I suspect, was close to the truth – heaven is close.

Heaven a Big Deal in Scripture

In the English Standard Version, the word 'heaven' appears 492 times in 463 verses and the word 'heavens' appears 203 times.

No surprise, and as we would expect it starts of course in the first book, Genesis, with 19 references. In my office I have a thick volume – *Doré's Illustrations* – large and full of beautiful etchings of Bible stories and characters. One of my favourites is a compelling illustration of Jacob's dream, where we see angels ascending and descending a stairway, and the Lord above it. Jacob wakes up and describes this moment as observing the 'gate of heaven'. As we would also expect, the last book, Revelation, is pregnant with references: 47 in all, beginning with John's grand entrance through the 'door' of heaven.

In the gospels there are 132 references to heaven, all from the lips of Jesus himself. Put into context, 27 per cent of all the references to the word heaven come from the lips of Jesus, the man who came from heaven, who talked about his father in heaven.[13] He promised Nathanael, 'Truly, truly, I say to you, you will see heaven opened, and the angels of God ascending and descending on the Son of man.'[14] In Acts we read, 'This Jesus, who was taken up from you into heaven, will come in the same way as you saw him go into heaven.'[15]

In contemporary language people often talk about going 'up to heaven', and it's common for us to think of angels coming 'down from heaven'; it appears scripture seems to support that notion. It's fair to say that with Jacob's dreamy glimpse and John's grand entrance, Jesus' words to Nathanael and the passage describing his ascension, we get this simple view of up to heaven and down from heaven.

It's as close as the cherubim with the flaming sword, as close as Jacob's gate, as close as John's door. On one level, then, closer than we think, and yet in terms of present accessibility further than we want.

In the most famous prayer in history, a prayer that was a step by step mentoring experience for the disciples, Jesus seems to be intent on impressing on the disciples and us the daily relevance, the daily importance and the daily impact of heaven on our lives. We'll develop this thought later, but it starts with the famous words uttered tens of thousands of times daily around the world, 'Our Father in heaven, hallowed be your name. Your kingdom come, your will be done, on earth as it is in heaven.'[17]

This choice of words is no accident. Jesus himself wanted heaven to be in the forefront of our thoughts on a daily basis and he wanted us to see, understand and then respond to the implications that God's will in heaven was to find expression in the here and now on earth. Everything done in heaven is connected with an ultimate purpose and an ultimate outcome on earth.

Heaven is God's Address

In various ways, scripture makes it clear heaven is God's place first and foremost. It's his location and the centre of his rule and activity. Its importance is not primarily about our destination after death, its importance is that it is where God lives and rules now.

The Israelite was to pray, 'Look down from your holy habitation, from heaven'.[18] God is 'the God of heaven'. He is also the, 'Possessor of heaven', 'Lord of heaven', 'heavenly Father' or 'Father in heaven'.[19]

God is not alone there, for we read of 'the host of heaven' which worships him[20] and of 'the angels in heaven'.[21] Those who are followers of Jesus may also look forward to an inheritance 'kept in heaven' for them.[22] Heaven is therefore the present address of God and his angels, and the ultimate destination of every disciple of Jesus.

It's not just God's address; he really does live there – now. For example, the prodigal son says, 'I have sinned against heaven,' meaning he has sinned against God and presumably God's companions in heaven.

Importantly, heaven is seen to be the place where God's throne is the central focus. We will pick this thread up in more detail later but, ultimately, nothing else approaches the singular importance of this one fact. This on its own would and should convince us that heaven is not primarily about us, it's about God the Father, God the Son and God the Holy Spirit. And praise God, because it is primarily about the Father, Son and Spirit, it includes us by design and intent. In his kindness, his love, his shepherding care, he ensures that heaven is also our individual hope and provides perspective and comfort for those left behind.

Heaven is also the sending base of the Holy Spirit and is the current location of the risen Jesus. According to Stephen at his martyrdom and according to the writer of Hebrews, he is 'at the right hand of God', 'at the right hand of the throne of the Majesty in heaven'.[23]

Think of it this way, God's throne is mentioned more than 40 times in Revelation, some in present heaven and some in the new heaven and new earth. John expresses it like this: 'After this I looked, and behold, a door standing open in heaven! And the first voice, which I had heard speaking to me like a trumpet, said, "Come up here, and I will show you what must take place after this." At once I was in the Spirit, and behold, a throne stood in heaven, with one seated on the throne.'[24] This throne is not a figure of speech it's a description of reality. All heaven revolves around the throne, and the Lamb is at the centre of that throne.

God's throne is central to heaven and, as we shall see, central to his purposes, his overarching connected purposes on earth.

CHAPTER 5

Two Places Called Heaven

———•———

It's a Bit Confusing at First

It's a puzzle for some of us, and yet it's such an intriguing, inspiring discovery when we see in scripture that there are two places called heaven. As we have seen, heaven is first and foremost God's address and it appears God intends to move. If it's true that when we die we don't go into an eternal coma but our Spirit is immediately with Jesus, where exactly do we go? It's rather like a final destination and a stopover. As I imagine we have all been taught, there is ultimately a new heaven and new earth which together form the final destination.

Our ultimate destination is an embodied resurrection in which, with fantastic new bodies like the body of Jesus himself, we inhabit a new heaven, a new earth and a wonderful new Jerusalem. The film *Space 1999* says in its trailer: 'New earth with a new Eden where you can begin again.' It's in the trailer because it resonates so deeply with our longings.

Randy Alcorn says: 'The power of Christ's resurrection is enough not only to remake us, but also to remake every inch of the universe – mountains, rivers, plants, animals, stars, nebulae, quasars, and galaxies. Christ's redemptive work extends resurrection to the far reaches of the universe.'[2] Alcorn also quotes Martin Luther, who once said, 'Our Lord has written the promise of the resurrection not in books alone, but in every leaf in springtime.'

Our current home, this wonderful planet is not destined to be discarded, it is essential to God's plan. God promises, 'as surely as I live that all the earth will be filled with the glory of the Lord'. In the beginning God formed, planted, built, and made, all in the first few pages of our Bible. In the last few pages we see him at work again in the magnificent best of the best – the new heaven and the new earth.

In *The Message* translation, Eugene Peterson paraphrases scripture to read: 'All the broken and dislocated pieces of the universe – people and things, animals and atoms – get properly fixed and fit together in vibrant harmonies, all because of his death, his blood that poured down from the cross.'[3]

Paula Gooder maintains that Paul believed, as do we, that 'resurrection is a load-bearing stone of faith'. Resurrection bodies are seen always in the New Testament to be bodies, and the model is what we see in Jesus and his post-resurrection body, which was recognizable even with nail prints. He was able to eat and drink, talk, move limitlessly, and yet able to defy current laws of physics by appearing and disappearing, and was apparently able to go through solid matter while still being able to be solid enough for the disciples to hold his feet, touch his hands and put their fingers into the wounds in his side. 'Marvellous body, oh wonderful, wonderful body, I long for you,' is the cry of my heart, and not mine alone. Romans 8, as we shall see, suggests that the whole of creation is crying out, longing for the redemption of its current state too. Thus it is that Christians believe we will experience the same kind of life beyond the grave that Jesus himself experienced. Paul makes this part crystal clear: in this life beyond the grave we will have bodies, and that is an essential part of the Christian faith.[4]

In 1 Corinthians 15 Paul talks about seeing the resurrected Christ, and he then goes on to describe our resurrection bodies. It's possible this was his road to Damascus experience but equally possible that it was when he was caught up into the third heaven. Either way it makes the case for the present heaven containing a risen, resurrected Jesus with an amazing body!

N.T. Wright calls the final destination after the intermediate state or present heaven 'life after "life after death"'. Life after death is therefore, and importantly, not all there is.[5] If we do not go straight to our final destination, where do we go at the moment when we die? N.T. Wright also suggests that when Jesus says, 'I go to prepare a place for you', the Greek word for 'place' *mone* is most often used for a temporary dwelling place, implying an eventual move to another location.

Present Heaven is a Stopover, Not the Final Destination

When I touched my dead son's body for the very last time, I placed my cheek against his still slightly warm bearded cheek and allowed myself to feel the gentle warmth. In the yawning chasm of loss that was abruptly opening up before me, a question was already forming. Where is Joel now then? Is he unconscious or is he truly in heaven? Why did God take him now? Surely the answer to those questions and more must be found in, where he has gone and what he is doing there?

We know that life after death, i.e. what happens immediately after we die, is not all that there is. We described it just now by saying there is a final destination and a stopover. I have travelled a good deal, often with Gill and one or more family members. On long-haul trips we often intentionally build in a stopover. The stopover frequently gets nearly as much attention – and there really are some great places to stopover – but you never forget that while this might be the best place you have visited so far, there is even better to come.

Imagine if on a planned vacation you got the stopover and final destination confused. Confused about where exactly you'd be staying, confused about the culture, confused about what there is to do, confused about who would be there and confused about the sights and sounds, and even the precise location of where you were supposed to be. It's a limited metaphor, I know, but instead of talking with joy, anticipation and thrill about both places, your conversations would be uncertain, muted, confused and lacklustre. It's another one of those reasons why Christians talk little and think little about heaven

So if, as we have suggested, the last breath here, the next breath somewhere else. Where exactly is that?

There's no better to starting point than the words of Jesus. On the cross, Jesus turned to one of the two thieves dying with him and said to him, 'Today you will be with me in Paradise.'[6]

A Stopover Called Paradise

Jesus gave the dying thief a promise, and that promise was personal and geographical. You are going to be with me and together we are going to be in a specific location called Paradise. Two thousand plus years later, and as you read this very sentence, the dying thief – I have no doubt – is still enjoying his paradise location with Jesus. Paul, in describing what was probably a Near Death Experience (NDE) or an out of body experience, uses the same Greek word for paradise to describe his visit to present heaven.[7] In Revelation, the apostle John uses the same word as he talks about 'the paradise of God', when he is clearly in present heaven.[8]

People reporting positive NDEs often describe the place they glimpsed as being like a beautiful garden. For the Christian, as soon as the spirit is released from the body by death it has direct access to the presence of the lord. It is a beautiful garden-like place, and Paul says it is better by far than the best we have here.

The idea of a walled garden, enclosing a carefully cultivated area of exquisite plants and animals, was the most powerful symbol of paradise available to the human imagination, mingling the images of beauty of nature with the orderliness of human construction... The whole human history is thus enfolded in the subtle interplay of sorrow over a lost paradise, and the hope of its final restoration.[9]

The personal and the geographical are the promise for every Christian who dies. Paradise is the name that Jesus, Paul and John give to the destination for Christians at death. The name Paradise comes from the Persian word for a pleasure garden, a walled garden, a place of design, a place of beauty, a place of peace and a place of joy. And that's why over the centuries many writers have used it when talking about the Garden of Eden. The Hanging Gardens of Babylon, with their sophisticated systems of irrigation, were one of the Seven Wonders of the Ancient World. They were so magnificently beautiful that people would travel from all over the world, just to catch a glimpse. Paradise is intended to get us longing for Eden-style beauty, our hearts skipping a beat at the thought of being there.

Just before he died, Roy Castle described a vision he was having, standing in a most beautiful garden. He said it was indescribable because it was more beautiful than any garden he had seen on earth. He added, 'I thought I was a gardener, but this gardener's something else!'[10]

I remember Joel's last moments on earth with us as if they were yesterday. Joel took advantage of these moments to prepare us, his family, with carefully thought through conversations, audio recordings for us to listen to later and practical preparation. Those moments were bittersweet; they were charged with unforgettable emotion, importance and impact. Jesus chooses a similar moment to prepare his disciples for the reality of their location after death. These words were carefully chosen words, preparing his friends, his closest ones, for his impending death and departure. He wanted to give his disciples and us something tangible to look forward to – an actual place, a geographical location, where they and we would go to be with him. Like the thief, he was giving the disciples a promise: it's both personal (he will be there to welcome us) and geographical – it's a real place.

Let not your hearts be troubled. Believe in God; believe also in me. In my Father's house are many rooms. If it were not so, would I have told you that I go to prepare a place for you?[11]

Here is a moment where the words would never be forgotten, like our moments with Joel, a bittersweet moment of high importance and high impact. And at that moment, Jesus deliberately chose everyday words, physical terms – house, rooms, place – to describe where he was going and what he was preparing for us. This stuff is real. Paradise is not somehow a metaphor: it's real, a place of stunning, gobsmacking beauty. Jesus has promised to be there and promised he has prepared a purpose-built place for us.

'I go to prepare a place for you'. This is a place designed for us by Jesus with a personal promise that touches the heart. This is a promise that adds strength to a future beyond this life that is different, better and purpose-made, purpose-built. Doubly meaningful to the disciples who, together with Jesus, were on the move. Doubly meaningful because it comes from the lips of Jesus who had nowhere to lay his head. This is a purpose-built place with a purpose-built location. That's why, as we see elsewhere in the book, 'I am always going home inside'. As we saw in Chapter 2, we can spiritualize these things and somehow perceive that they are less than real and in so doing we lose the wonder of the place and lose our longing to be there.

After visiting paradise Paul called what he saw 'surpassing greatness'. To be with Christ is better by far – that's not a dry theological dogma, that's a sensory explosion better than anything we have ever seen or could ever imagine. If it's better by far, if it is a place of 'surpassing greatness', then expect to be blown away. By definition Paul's use of 'surpassing greatness' and 'better by far' again points to the reality that paradise is not a metaphor, not an analogy, it's a place of breathtaking greatness.

Please don't tell yourself that the garden called paradise is no better than your garden. Please don't ever believe even for a second that the most spectacular views you have enjoyed in forests, mountains, valleys, canyons, oceans and in the skies are the best. No! Those wonderful experiences are not the reality, they are the shadow, the pale reflection of the real thing.

Paradise More Beautiful than Anything You Have Ever Seen

What is it that feeds our souls on earth? It's a kaleidoscope of ingredients. The work we do, when it has meaning and does others good. Colour, light, the natural world, variety, scale, shape and form. Then add to that the limitless creativity of human endeavour, from the scale of construction like pyramids, to aircraft like the jumbo jet and Concorde, to thatched cottages, design, art and sculpture, exploration of other worlds. We are made for it, drawn to it, it is as if it almost calls to us. Then there is eating, drinking and fine dining. The exquisite process that goes into making then storing wines and champagnes. There is the milk of human kindness that we experience in friendships and family. There are moments of love, joy and peace that build us, entrance us, captivate us. Imagine paradise, then, as all that on steroids!

I love the natural world and have always been drawn to beauty. Some beauty on this earth is simply breathtaking, even with all its imperfection. My wife and I love to snorkel, and we have been to some wonderful places such as the Bahamas, the Florida Keys and notably the Red Sea. Some friends who are experienced divers took us to one stretch of the Red Sea near Sharm El Sheikh and they warned us of the underwater cliff-edge drop a few metres from the shoreline. I can remember the moment as if were yesterday: the breathtaking drop, the clarity of the water to seemingly impossible depths, the countless varieties of fish and sea creatures. It was beautiful enough to draw a tear of gratitude. We have watched the Attenborough nature documentaries and the 'Blue Planet' series, along with countless other natural world documentaries over the years with awe.

Gill and I celebrated our fortieth wedding anniversary with a series of safaris across five Kenyan game parks. The things we saw, the birds, the predators, the Big Five, natural beauty, sunsets and sunrises, were awe-inspiring. Mount Kilimanjaro calling with its snow-capped beauty, and the amazing sight not just of individual animals but the jaw-dropping encounters with thousands of elephants and tens of thousands of wildebeest gave a glimpse of unimaginable scale.

I sail a fair bit and get to see beautiful night skies with no night pollution, a sunrise where for a few seconds the sun almost fills half the sky. I recall my first ever celestial navigation lesson, where tears ran down my face as I 'brought the sun down to the horizon' using an instrument called a sextant. That moment was a moment of connection for me with my creator and the creator of heaven and earth. These are a tiny taste on the tip of our beauty appreciation taste buds. Heaven has to be more and has to be better.

Please don't tell me heaven has none of this. Please don't suggest that what heaven has will somehow be boring, set up like a Sunday gathering. Please don't suggest to me that heaven will somehow be less breathtaking. This is God's address, God's place, God's home. Eye has not seen, nor ear heard half of what God has prepared for those who love him. Think of the best places on this planet, the best sunsets, the best mountain views, the best of 'Blue Planet' above and below the water, the best natural world experiences and the best natural parks you've ever visited. They are nothing, nothing, hear it, believe it, nothing compared to paradise. There will be music like we've never heard before, light like we've never seen it before, construction that will make world-class buildings like Notre Dame or Westminster Abbey look like sandcastles, beauty more breathtaking than anything we could imagine. And it starts with his welcome, his arms wide open in a welcome home embrace. 'Welcome home!'

Earth is not the best there is. It's wonderful, but it is less than, second string, not as good as all that is to come. Death is not the end of all that is precious, it's the doorway to the very best there is. Death is the doorway to the greatest adventure. Expect your God-given senses to reel and reel again as you travel to the next world and get to see perfect nature, perfect art, design and construction and perfected relationships.

Some stopovers are famous for the sights, the natural beauty of the place. Others are famous for who you might see. Paradise is the very best of both. I can't wait!

CHAPTER 6

Paradise: The Official Tour Guide

———•———

Our final destination we have seen is in a resurrection body in a new city with a new earth and a new heaven. Paradise – present heaven – is a stopover; so what can we expect from our wonderful but temporary stopover.

Many times in our married life Gill and I have travelled for vacation to a new location, we have purchased the 'official' tour guide well ahead of our departure to ensure we were as prepared as we could possibly be, and to feed our current day to day, the humdrum, with anticipation of what is to come. These official tour guides are dependable and are not sponsored by advertising. Any hyperbole written is trustworthy and in our years of vacation to wonderful places as varied as Disneyland and Rome, Florida and Singapore, our experience has been informed, clarified and enhanced by reading the descriptions of someone who has been there before, and wants to share all that we might expect. Information in these tour guides typically includes location and travel plans, things to see, culture, natural wonders, what others wear and who might be there.

So it is that the best descriptions, the most reliable descriptions of paradise, are going to be from sources that are utterly reliable and from sources who have been there. This chapter then, is given over to three people who have been to paradise, and whose words and descriptions appear in the canon of scripture. This chapter will reflect thoughts from the writings of Jesus, the apostle John and the apostle Paul, with some additional contributors in the form of Stephen, Ezekiel and Elisha. Together they give us the official version of what to anticipate and how best to prepare.

A Different Reality

Paradise is real, as real as the device or the paper you are holding in your hands. Real in every sense: it is a physical location, it has living people inhabiting it, it is full of natural wonders, and best of all it's actually God's home. But it's different too. You can't see it unless God opens your eyes for a moment or takes you there.

In Acts, in what was arguably an NDE (Near Death Experience), Stephen was in what the Celts called a 'thin place' – a place and a moment in time where heaven opens in the present and the immediate. There was a throne and Jesus was standing there. It was not a vision or an impression, a picture or a prophetic sensing, it was real, immediate and powerful enough to sustain him in his horrific and tortuous last moments. This was not a metaphor. God opened his eyes to a dimension of reality that others in scripture have seen, but which is hidden from most of us most of the time.

Elisha prays for Gehazi's eyes to be opened to 'see'. And when his eyes were opened, he saw horses, chariots and angelic warriors. He was privileged for that moment to see some of the hosts of heaven and the reality of their engagement with things on earth.[1] These things too were not a picture, a metaphor, a parable – they were glimpses of the real thing.

This is a different kind of reality. Both Stephen and Gehazi are part of a historical narrative in scripture and neither of these stories can be construed as storytelling or parables. These horses and chariots, like Jacob's ladder, like Stephen's glimpse of heaven are probably representative of the reality that, yes, while hidden from most of us for most of the time, there is a real heaven, and Jesus is really there. This heaven is closer than we might imagine. And already in our tour guide we are discovering this world is active and, just like God himself, is engaged with, inextricably linked with and connected to our world. It may just be hidden close by in our own universe or 'in a universe near you'.

Paradise as Seen by Paul

We get another glimpse of the same reality of paradise from Paul's own experience. Paul's third heaven encounter deeply impacted him, and of course inspired many verses including four that we looked at earlier on the theme that 'to live is Christ, to die is gain'. Let's read his text:

> I know a man in Christ who fourteen years ago was caught up to the third heaven – whether in the body or out of the body I do not know, God knows. And I know that this man was caught up into paradise – whether in the body or out of the body I do not know, God knows ... and he heard things that cannot be told, which man may not utter. On behalf of this man I will boast, but on my own behalf I will not boast, except of my weaknesses. Though if I should wish to boast, I would not be a fool, for I would be speaking the truth. But I refrain from it, so that no one may think more of me than he sees in me or hears from me. So to keep me from becoming conceited because of the surpassing greatness of the revelations, a thorn was given me in the flesh, a messenger of Satan to harass me, to keep me from becoming conceited. Three times I pleaded with the Lord about this, that it should leave me. But he said to me, 'My grace is sufficient for you, for my power is made perfect in weakness.' Therefore I will boast all the more gladly of my weaknesses, so that the power of Christ may rest upon me.[2]

It's interesting that he was not sure if it was his spirit that went or his body. It's as if he is uncertain what his form was. It was like a body but clearly not exactly the same as his earthly body. This presents us with a theological challenge: do we have a body in paradise or will we be some form of spiritual being? There are different schools of thought here. All are agreed that in paradise we do not yet have our resurrection body, but it's equally clear from Paul and John's descriptions that we exist in a manner that allows sensations, walking, clothing, function and are recognizable. Paul can't be absolutely clear what this form is and, interestingly, when doing their best to describe God himself and his heavenly beings, a number of Old Testament writers had a similar challenge describing what they saw. For instance:

> the Ancient of Days took his seat;
> his clothing was white as snow,
>   and the hair of his head like pure wool;
> his throne was fiery flames;
>   its wheels were burning fire.[3]

and behold a man clothed in linen, with a belt of fine gold from Uphaz around his waist. His body was like beryl, his face like the appearance of lightning, his eyes like flaming torches, his arms and legs like the gleam of burnished bronze, and the sound of his words like the sound of a multitude.[4]

In these passages, Daniel is grappling with a similar challenge, and he describes what he saw in terms of a body with function, but a body that had a form very different to his own body. For this reason and for the sake of simplifying the concept, I am surmising that in paradise we have a form of body, different in nature to both our natural body and our ultimate resurrection body but nonetheless with form that relates in some way to the attributes we expect a body to have. We could put it another way: when we die, we have shape and form; it's not our resurrection body yet, but as Paul has described it in this way it's reasonable to call our shape and form a body. It carries the traits that bodies carry. Paul could see, hear and presumably talk. The fact that Elijah and Moses could be seen and identified lends credence to the reality of some kind of body. And many, either in NDEs or in that twilight zone between death and life talk about relatives that they recognize. That recognition implies that those who have already arrived in paradise have bodies.

Paul not being sure of whether he was in the body or out has to suggest something striking. Twice he makes the point. This in itself maybe a clue as to how our spirits are clothed in the present heaven. It certainly implies that whatever our form in heaven it feels like the body we have inhabited, does things like the body we have inhabited, and therefore has some of the functions and capabilities of the body we are in right now. But it also makes clear that this shape, this form, this body is different.

Paul also describes what he saw with extravagant words: 'the surpassing greatness of the revelations'.[5] His experience was so life changing, so impacting that he is given a thorn in his flesh to keep him from going there. This is not dull heaven, this is not boring heaven, this is real heaven full of real adventure and real mystery. Paul deliberately uses the word paradise, which confirms the location of this NDE or out of body experience. It's where the dying thief is today; it is the present heaven. We observe that he hears things which 'cannot be told', 'which man cannot utter'. It's as if he has been told or has deduced that he mustn't share the detail of things he has seen. Why is that? It's clear that it's partly due to the surpassing greatness of it all. This place is great it's beyond great and maybe he knew that if he kept sharing the detail it would potentially rob him of the unfulfilled apostolic work he was yet to do. It obviously impacted him so greatly that the compass needle of his longing from then on always pointed to the magnetic pull of paradise. 'I desire (long) to be with Christ', 'to die is gain', 'it is better by far'. The experience has changed him forever. And rather like the astronauts who have visited the moon returning with rock samples, Paul gives us tantalizingly attractive glimpses of stardust from paradise to make us gasp in wonder.

During his experience, first there is this significant 'great revelation' conversation. Together with what we know from Ezekiel of the activity around the throne and Jacob's ladder we can deduce that this significant conversation is linked to significant activity, which for most of us, most of the time is hidden from us for our good and presumably for the good of the advancement of the kingdom. We will do our best to develop this theme in Chapter 7.

This experience would have undoubtedly informed Paul's scriptures on resurrection and resurrection body theology. I don't know if you have observed this trait with preachers: they will often tell a story and give a fictitious name so that the congregation cannot make out who the person is. However, it is comically common for some details to slip out innocently in the story, so that a big chuckle ripples across the congregation as they have clocked who the story is about.

So while Paul cannot utter the detail overtly in one go, it has to have informed much of his writing. I think when we read 1 Corinthians 15, 1 Thessalonians 4 and Philippians, we don't have to look far to see that it is infused with the reality of what he saw, heard and experienced. He could have told us so much more. If it was the case that even after fourteen years of reflection and prayer he was still unsure about the precise nature of the 'body' in heaven, then it's okay for us not to know for certain. Not just okay, but for some reason God himself seems to keep much of the detail hidden, unspoken, unwritten. Scripture does however allow enough to build a general picture, with some of the clues being quite clear.

In his Damascus road conversion, Paul saw a light from heaven and heard a voice also from heaven, so this is a man, an apostle, who has been exposed directly to heaven's touch at least twice in his adult life. And of course, it is this experience that puts credibility to his words repeated elsewhere in this book: 'For to me to live is Christ, and to die is gain'; 'My desire is to depart and be with Christ, for that is far better'.

Notice how the experience also causes him to contrast this world with the next: the next is gain, the next is to be with Christ, the next is better by far! The challenge for us with Paul and with the apostle John is that they tell us things which are not always clearly delineated. Some of the things they share apply to only the new heaven and the new earth, some are just for paradise and some appear to be in both.

From his experience, Paul begins to unpack what our resurrection bodies will look like and I imagine that he got glimpses of this in paradise. I have listed the main thoughts he develops below:[6]

- recognizable
- different
- imperishable
- glorious
- powerful
- spiritual
- changed

Recognizable

I shared earlier in this book Gill's fears about heaven early on in our marriage. One of those fears was that she worried she wouldn't know how to find me in heaven. We actually dealt with this by agreeing to meet at Peter's house, a location that we both felt we could find! Interestingly, over the years I have discovered that behind that fear is a commonly asked question, will we be recognizable in heaven? Eric Clapton's song 'Tears in Heaven' expresses the same concern where he asks the question of his 4-year-old son, effectively wanting to be reassured that his son would recognize him if they met in heaven.

Thankfully, the Bible gives us real glimpses of people beyond the grave, and always implicitly affirms continuity of individuality and personality, answering with clarity and certainty that we will be recognizable, and we will recognize our loved ones. In Paul's illustration, the wheat seed becomes the wheat ear, transformed and yet the same.[7] When Jesus appeared in his resurrected body, he was recognizable and yet also clearly different. Somehow there was continuity of his person and he was recognizable, and yet also with wonderful transformation.

David expected to meet his son in Sheol and stopped praying once he was dead. He prayed and fasted for his son's healing but was reconciled with the fact he would meet him and know him in death.[8] In the very bizarre account of Samuel being made visible to Saul and the witch of Endor, he was clearly recognizable.[9] In the text, quite remarkably he is described as old and wearing a robe. Interestingly, in this story the witch was in terror and it was Samuel that spoke, not the witch acting as medium. I mention that here because some have understood God to be endorsing or allowing an activity here, which elsewhere, he prohibits – that of consulting a medium. In this case and on the mount of transfiguration, it was more likely God himself who called Samuel and, certainly, it was God himself who placed Moses and Elijah onto the earth. Mediums conjure up evil spirits which purport to be voices from the dead. The witch of Endor got a shock because what came up was not an evil spirit under her control but the power of God bringing up Samuel himself. More significantly, because of the time lapse, Moses and Elijah came as themselves at the mount of transfiguration.[10] This transfiguration involved the recognizable bodies of Elijah and Moses. They were talking and walking, so while they are clearly not the final resurrection bodies, they were nonetheless in some form of evidently identifiable form that looked like bodies. Peter, James and John recognized them. That in itself is remarkable, as they had obviously never met them, there were no name labels, and they had no art, iPhotos or WhatsApp to check them out.

We've already mentioned the story of Lazarus. This is a Jesus story and it's a story with names, including Lazarus and Abraham. All the participants had names, they had functions normally attributable to bodies, including awareness, thirst, tongues, heat. They recognized each other. In the gospels Jesus talks about the God of Abraham, Isaac and Jacob as the God of the living, not the dead – the named, recognizable living. Gill needn't have worried after all.

Different, Imperishable, Glorious, Powerful, Spiritual

While referring specifically to the resurrected body Paul describes the body in death: 'It is sown in dishonour; it is raised in glory. It is sown in weakness; it is raised in power.' When my father died, I recall the shocking indignity as he was lowered into a metal casket by two men. In most cultures, dead bodies are covered over with sheets to shield onlookers from the painful, shocking or unpleasant experience of looking on a corpse. The longer time goes on, the less we want to look. Paul describes how the body is sown in weakness and raised in strength. In Joel's brutally fast illness, his body got weaker and weaker. I have a wonderful picture of him and me together in early September with his torso looking fit and his magnificent biceps bulging as we worked in his garden together. By December, his arms were so thin the medics needed a paediatric cuff to measure his blood pressure. There were days where he could stand for just a few minutes, all his body could manage, rest his head on my shoulder and cry out, 'Oh Dad!' The weakness was so debilitating for him. He had been such an active person, climbing, fishing, hunting, walking, working. What a joy, a thrill to know that right now he is in paradise in a body with magnificent shape, magnificent form and eternally gifted strength.

Right now, Jesus is in paradise with a resurrected body that can walk through doors. The stone was rolled away to let disciples in, not to let Christ out! He was raised a spiritual body but this spiritual body could still be touched. It had flesh and bones, it could eat, and the nail prints and the wound were still present, really present so that Thomas could put his fingers in the gaps. This is Jesus appearing as he was but also different. He cooked and ate fish at the seashore, but there were observable remarkable differences. He could play hide and seek with his appearance with the disciples en route to Emmaus. He could disappear from them and appear in the upper room, arriving in sci-fi style through walls. And it seems in paradise, even in our pre-resurrection bodies we shall be able to move in a new way, rather similar to the way Jesus did. Daniel describes angels coming swiftly in the evening flight, which may well be a function of our paradise bodies.

What is also clear is that while we are recognizable, there is something very different about our bodies. In Revelation we read: 'they will walk with me in white, for they are worthy. The one who conquers will be clothed thus in white garments, and I will never blot his name out of the book of life.'[12]

You can't walk without feet. Whatever is dressed, by implication has form and is therefore some form of body. However, it's a spiritual body. The glimpse we have taken already of the transfiguration was of bright white clothing, and in the case of Jesus a changed face, which in the text appears to suggest glorious light. Daniel refers to shining like the brightness of the heavens, like the stars forever. Jesus, presumably leaning on Daniel's words, tells us that the righteous will shine like the sun in the kingdom of their father. Angels in the gospel stories appear in dazzling white. Expect better bodies with better attributes and better abilities and expect to be dressed in dazzling white; a 'Persil eat your heart out' kind of white. A white that dazzles with purity and illumination. Even before our final resurrection body, this is wonderful change, dazzling white change, heart-stopping, soul-lifting change. These all new pre-resurrection paradise-inhabiting 'bodies' hide no darkness; gone are the shadows as they reflect the glorious nature of God, the glorious character of God and the wonderful meaningful purpose of God. 'When he appears, we shall be like him, because we shall see him as he is.'[13] Paul says 'we shall also bear the likeness of the man of heaven.'[14]

I know my body. It's creaking at the seams and has an insatiable desire and tendency to drag me towards the darkness, towards sin and towards decay. My natural tendencies are to be fearful, lazy, disobedient and wilful. Where, oh where is this heavenly body? I long to be clothed with it. A body which responds to the desires, the promptings and purposes of God. A new body or form which, albeit temporary, is adamant that it will follow God, is clothed only in light, and has no shadow of sinful turning. Oh heavenly form, what a promise, what a joy! This paradise body doesn't creak, groan or get old, it doesn't get sick or sad. This paradise body is made of the stuff of eternal life, which instinctively bends to the will of the Father. I think Paul longed for it and I do too. This paradise body has nothing shameful or deceitful, it's full of light and it radiates light.

In 1 Corinthians, Paul suggests we shall know fully, even as we are fully known.[15] In the presence of the Way, the Truth and the Life, we will also be exposed to truth facts knowledge, and the fullness of heaven's perspective. There is continuity of knowledge and consciousness. My grandson Jacob gave an amazing tribute to his dad at the cremation, and he remarked that his dad had said, 'I will have all the answers and no questions; you will have all the questions and no answers'. And although Joel probably said that to Jacob slightly tongue-in-cheek, the reality is that we have both consciousness and knowledge after death. In the story of Lazarus and the rich man there is clearly consciousness for the rich man, as he recalls his five brothers and pleads for action on their behalf. There will be no doubt in our minds that we have just moved from one place to another.

Paradise as Described by the Apostle John

The apostle John had a form of body in his heavenly taster tour too. He doesn't describe it except by inference: he took hold of things, ate things, saw things, spoke, fell prostrate, heard and even wrote. As we saw just now, in Paul's visit, it was as if Paul sensed he had a body but it wasn't like his normal body. John, even more than Paul, develops the things that will mark our new home. Some of these attributes will be fully appreciated in the new heaven and new earth but all have a part in paradise.

Who will be there? All of God's people, from the Garden of Eden to the present day. Millions upon millions of the saints. Every tribe, tongue and nation represented. Legions of angels will be there, together with archangels, cherubim and seraphim. The heavenly host, including the angels that sang or spoke the announcement to the shepherds at the birth of Jesus, the angels present in the wilderness temptation and at the tomb will be there. Of course, the star attraction, the Lord God Almighty and the Lamb are there. All your Bible heroes and heroes of the faith down the ages will be there. And there is every reason to expect they will be knowable and accessible. Who would you most like to talk to? What questions will you ask? I would love to see Adam and Eve, and see for myself what the first creation looks like. I would love to chat with Jesus, with Prime Minister Joseph, with Peter, with Nathaniel and then Nathan the prophet, and countless others.

And of course, all your Christian family and friends will be there. All the goodbyes will now lead to fresh hellos, with eternity to catch up and then create new memories and adventures together for ever. No fear of a parting to tinge or spoil the pleasure. I can't wait to see my dad, my mum, and of course my son, my best friend. And knowing Joel he'll have something memorable planned for everyone in the family upon their arrival. Joel said to the family once, 'There has never been a bad conversation over a good bottle of wine.' He also said the same over great champagnes. I don't know if there's champagne in heaven, I can't imagine paradise without, but we do know from the lips of Jesus as well as John that there will be wine. Imagine that heavenly wine, fine and rare wine – what a bouquet, what a taste, what an experience to share with family and friends, and what conversations we shall have there.

The Tree of Life is There

What is clear is that this is not some wild place of unruly nature; this indicates some kind of cultivation. It's a place of exquisite natural beauty, with plants, and likely animals too. The Garden of Eden was apparently not destroyed after the fall, but the entrance was blocked, and it was blocked presumably to ensure that no one would get to the tree of life. I'm not aware, even in movies, that anyone has ever claimed to have found this first garden.

Fast-forward the stopover tour guide to heaven and see in Revelation that the tree of life is presently in paradise. The chances are high that it's not the only tree, and John explicitly promises those who overcome the right to eat from the tree of life.[16] Three times this wonder tree is mentioned in the Garden of Eden, once in the present heaven and three times in the new heaven and new earth. This tree is doubly significant in that Adam and Eve were driven from it and cherubim with a flaming sword that turned every way were placed there to guard the way to the tree of life. Adam and Eve were driven out so that they could not live forever in their newly acquired sinful state and now, millennia later, it's there for those who have gone to paradise to eat from it. Wonderful taste, eternal life-giving properties. Who needs five a day!

It's interesting that angels and even God in human disguise could eat food, as we see with Abraham under the oaks at Mamre.[17] Food and drink were really important to the risen Jesus, eating fish in the upper room and setting up a barbeque on the beach for the disciples. Talking about the new heaven and new earth, Isaiah says that 'On this mountain the LORD of hosts will make for all peoples a feast of rich food, a feast of well-aged wine, of rich food full of marrow, of aged wine well refined.'[18] And yes of course the specifics are for the new heaven and new earth, but very likely for paradise too. This is a paradise of celebration, a paradise of banquets, with the best of meats and wines.

Together with Paul and Jesus, John also describes what will be there and what will not be there. To be clear here, the bulk of these scriptures are weighted towards the new heaven and the new earth, and yet the inference is that these things probably in their breadth also apply to paradise.

What there will not be:[19]

- sea
- sorrow – wipe away all tears
- suffering
- temple or religion
- sun or moon
- sin
- night
- separation

What there will be:[20]

- shelter
- reward offered by Jesus
- responsibility creativity ruling over cities
- revelation knowing God as he is known
- righteousness – constant goodness
- place of rejoicing and celebration parties suppers banquets
- recognition
- rest

Some of these attributes we have reflected on already in this chapter, others we will pick up in the final chapters. I think it is helpful to reflect further here on one or two attributes.

We know that relationships continue. Paul, in 1 Corinthians, talks about love as an abiding eternal virtue. We will move into relationships that have undiluted, pure love, in every case and with everyone. We will see all that is good, wholesome, pure, unique and wonderful about those we love. There will be no sin, no temptation and no sinful nature to contaminate the experiences we will share – no shadows of any kind.

Feelings also continue. Think of your purest and greatest joy in this life on earth, multiply it by many times, remove all traces of darkness and self and you have feelings as God intended. Great joy, adoration and worship, contentment, satisfaction and peace. In his Psalm David, presumably with a glimpse of this, writes: 'In your presence there is fullness of joy; at your right hand there are pleasures for evermore'.[21] There is pleasure in paradise – real pleasure, untainted uncorrupted pleasure – and you and I will feel it all with a new intensity.

No more crying. There are tears on every continent, in every country on each continent and in every family that walks this earth. Think of the tears you have shed, seen, read about or watched on the news this week alone. The horror of ethnic cleansings, the brutality of war, the trauma of sex slavery. The pain of a child's grazed knee, the cry from an orphan's heart, the night-time tears of the newly widowed. Broken hearts in relationships, in family break ups, in bereavements. We live in a world saturated with tears. Those tears come from myriad sources and for a host of reasons, but come they do. I watched as Joel's wife, his son and daughter, and his mother wept over the suffering and pain. And I wept myself then and since, over and over.

The pain of separation brings tears too. Whether that's the brokenness of marriage relationships that separate families or even the more positive but nonetheless painful moments when members of the family move away and we only see them occasionally. Those moments of meeting up are sweet, but tinged already with the painful awareness of impending parting. All that changes – no more partings, no more unwanted geographical separation. 'No sea' is only mentioned in the context of the old earth and heaven. The first heaven and the first earth have passed away along with the *first* sea. Just making the point that everything about our Blue Planet is gone. It doesn't mean there are no bodies of water, rather there is no unwanted geographical separation, and all the pollution and damage done to our current oceans is gone and everything is made new. Bodies of water do appear in Revelation, and none more attractive than the river of life. If you are into water sports don't worry, there's enough water for you.

No more suffering, no more pain no more sickness! Death is gone, pain is gone, unkindness and spite are gone. Think of an eternal life free from anxiety, financial worries relational stress. Free from slipped discs, migraines, cancers, surgery and accidents traumas. Think of that same eternal life free from insecurity free from emotional pain, free from hurtful words and hurtful things. What a place to be; little wonder using the words of Paul again, this is *better by far*.

He wipes away our tears. Does that mean Jesus himself with a celestial Kleenex wipes tears from our face? Maybe, but that would suggest tears will keep on coming. It's more likely that as we see all the events of earth through the lens of God's plan and heaven's purpose, he will wipe away all tears for ever. For ever! Looking at every situation from God's viewpoint, we will see, we will understand, and we will be at peace.

There's no temple or sanctuary. There are no church meetings, services or religion in paradise. The Lamb is there, the place is lit up by his light. Authentic, Christ-centred living takes on a whole new level of meaning. The light of his presence will surround us wherever we are, wherever we go and whatever we do for eternity. This is authentic worship and authentic work in the unstoppable light of his presence. Jesus to serve, Jesus to worship and Jesus to be with forever, with no spoilers.

We now see why our heavenly Father is called both heavenly and father. Ephesians tells us that our Father in heaven is the one from whom every family in heaven and on earth is named.[22] Think on that! Every family in heaven and on earth – everyone, including you, is named after their heavenly Father. This a glimpse into the eternal importance of family and its continuity in heaven, and the importance of being named and, by inference, recognized by name. This should cause Eric Clapton to sing with joy. This is eternal family at work, not religion. We've taught it and tasted it in small measure in our church life on earth. Now we move into the fullness of family life and being with an accessible heavenly Father who will dwell for ever with his creatures, renewed relationships with our Christian earthly family, and renewed relationships for ever with the family of God.

John also begins to open our eyes to the breadth of our new home. In Revelation, in the present heaven we see martyrs wearing clothes, we see horses going in and out, there are trumpets, censers, smoke, people with palm branches in their hands, there are birds and there are creatures, as well as angels. There are riders, diadems, robes. We also get a glimpse of the scale and sound of words and worship. We read that he 'heard a voice from heaven that sounded like a roaring waterfall, like a loud peal of thunder. It sounded like the music made by musicians playing their harps.'[23] Imagine a voice that takes three angles of expression to convey the experience: roaring water, thunder and harps. What a sound, what a voice and what bodies are needed to hear that! John goes on to record: 'I heard what seemed to be the voice of a great multitude, like the roar of many waters and like the sound of mighty peals of thunder, crying out, "Hallelujah! For the Lord our God the Almighty reigns."'[24]

In Revelation 6, John narrates the story of the martyrs who are under the altar. There are various different interpretations of what this is actually defining, however looking at the passage:[25]

- they wear clothes
- there is question and answer with God
- they pray
- they are aware of what's going on earth
- they clearly have personal identity and memory

- they are conscious
- they are engaged in the purposes of God

Jesus Describes Our Paradise Home

Jesus told his disciples, 'In my father's house are many rooms. If it were not so, would I have told you that I go to prepare a place for you?'[26] As we saw in the previous chapter, in a moment of high importance and high impact Jesus deliberately chose everyday words, physical terms – house, rooms, place – to describe where he was going and what he was preparing for us These words were his words, words of promise, words of practical paradise promise, giving his disciples and us today something tangible to look forward to – an actual place, a promised place and a carefully prepared place where they and we would go to be with him.

In a plethora of TV programmes, like *Grand Designs* or *Love it or List It*, the presenters go to great lengths to understand the life and lifestyle likes and dislikes of the individual or families that want a change of location or a renewed version of their current home. Each programme is intent on ensuring that the finished outcome is especially tailored to the occupants, or in the case of *Grand Designs* tracking the progress of couples who have designed their own 'ideal home'. These reality TV shows trace the importance of a place called home and simply reflect the desire of the human heart for that home to 'suit me'. In an even grander way, paradise has physical places prepared for us and they will be home. Not just any home, but a truly grand design tailored for each one of us, and the creator of the universe has taken personal responsibility for where they are and what they look like. There is no place like home, and there has never been a place so uniquely designed for you and me like this home.

Jesus talked about heaven and peppered his conversation with the word. Altogether in the gospels the word appears more than 120 times, mostly from the lips of the Carpenter. He talked about the kingdom of heaven and reward in heaven. He talked about his father in heaven, he talked about reclining at table with the patriarchs in heaven, and talked about laying up treasure in heaven. Heaven was a focus and heaven was a passion.

In Chapter 8 we will reflect on this further, but Jesus, more than anyone, demonstrated the unity of heaven and earth and the importance of the interaction between heaven and earth. In the Lord's Prayer he wanted us to remember heaven every day, and in particular he wanted us to pray to his Father in heaven and to pray, 'Your kingdom come, your will be done, on earth as it is in heaven.' Jesus was making it clear that heaven was a real place, with a real heavenly Father, with a real responsibility to carry out heaven's wishes, heaven's strategies here on earth.

In the story of Lazarus and the rich man,[27] we get a glimpse into how we travel to heaven. The poor man died and was carried by angels to Abraham's side.

So it is that while relatives sorrow on earth, you will find yourself immediately in new surroundings, which just now are beyond our imagination. You will probably have seen angels who have been assigned the responsibility of escorting you to your destination, just as the angels carried Lazarus into Abraham's bosom. As we shall see in a few pages, many NDE accounts cite the presence of angels at the point of departure and or arrival into heaven.

There was a story that gripped my imagination in my early teenage years, and contributed to my own determination to follow God. In 1956, five young missionaries were speared to death in the jungles of Ecuador. The offenders have subsequently become Christians and told Steve Saint, son of one of the martyrs, that they heard and saw what they now believe to be angels while the killings were taking place. A woman hiding in the distance also saw these beings above the trees and didn't know what the music was until many years later when she heard a Christian choir on an album.[28]

When Elijah is taken up he too, apparently, is accompanied by angelic beings with chariots of fire and horses of fire as he goes up by a whirlwind. While not explicitly described, the inference is that angelic activity is involved. When Jesus ascends into heaven, two angels are present in white robes, and they take this opportunity to give some clarification and to bring illumination to the disciples so they know where he has gone, how he has got there and how he will return.

A Paradise to Die For

We glibly talk about a holiday to die for, or a meal to die for, but present heaven paradise really *is* to die for. And I know it may seem a little superficial but just for a moment think about a well-known scripture with me: 'he will give you the desires of your heart.'[27]

I know there are all kind of caveats around such a scripture, but think of it for a moment just in terms of life after death – what would your heart's desire be? Pause reading with me for a moment. If the afterlife could include anything you would love, what would you put there?

Let me guess just some of the things you are likely to have imagined:

- seeing and living with Jesus
- no sin
- no regrets
- no sickness
- no tears
- beautiful landscapes
- fantastic food and wine
- community
- unparalleled beauty with precious stones
- being reunited with all our loved ones
- pain removed
- questions and challenges answered
- the ability to know everyone there
- unlimited time to have conversations with biblical people and history makers
- unimaginable new adventures

These bullet points describe things that are real, tangible, physical. If we persist in the false notion that heaven is a spiritual place, i.e. non-physical, most of us find a heaven like that unimaginable. If we can't imagine it, we can't look forward to it.

But, as it is written:

> 'What no eye has seen,
>   nor ear heard,
> nor the heart of man imagined,
>   what God has prepared for those who love him' –

these things God has revealed to us through the Spirit.[30]

As previously mentioned, people reporting positive near-death experiences often describe the place they glimpsed as being like a beautiful garden. For the Christian, as soon as the spirit is released from the body by death, it has direct access to the presence of the Lord. It is a beautiful garden-like place and Paul says it is better by far than the best we have here. And from the utterly reliable source of scripture, our tour guides have already made clear what we can expect:

- heaven is a definite place – real geographical existence
- home
- destination
- tree of life

- God to be enjoyed there
- reward
- no sickness
- no tears
- no suffering
- water of life
- no poverty
- no sorrow
- no separation
- no death
- no sin
- everything new
- purposeful

That's great and awe-inspiring. What might other sources have to say?

CHAPTER 7

Paradise: The Trip Advisor Reviews

———

In the previous chapter, we made clear that the only totally reliable source for what we know about present heaven is the scripture itself. And we have spent time looking in particular at Paul, John and Jesus.

In scripture we also get details of 'experiences' that we might class as NDEs. Stephen, at the point of 'departure' whilst being stoned, saw Jesus and the throne in heaven presumably seconds before he actually died. Many commentators believe that when Paul was caught up into paradise it was at the moment of his stoning in Lystra, where he had been dragged out of the city, 'pronounced' dead. That could count as an NDE too.

We know, then, that Stephen saw Jesus and the throne in heaven before he died, and if Paul actually died and was caught up into paradise, or taken there in some other way, it is of course plausible that other Christians over the centuries will have had – and in this generation likely are still having – similar experiences. Reports of seeing heaven, of being taken there, of seeing Jesus or relatives long dead might just have some validity. Others in scripture like Ezekiel, Isaiah, Jacob and Gehazi get a glimpse of the heavenly realm at moments of crisis. And while these are not NDEs they are helpful, valuable and comforting 'glimpses', 'revelations', 'dreams' – and again it is highly plausible that other Christians will have similar experiences. I have included a few of these. It's interesting that John Bunyan is probably the most famous of this latter category.

Born in 1628, an Anglican tinker's son, Bunyan turned nonconformist minister. He composed the bestseller *Pilgrims Progress* while in prison for illegal preaching. Until the nineteenth century, this allegorical drama of a journey from the city of destruction to the heavenly city was the most popular English book after the Bible. Bunyan got his extended glimpses into heaven from a dream. Just one quotation might whet the appetite, give us a 'trip advisor review' from the 1600s, and remind us again that it is entirely plausible that God would use dreams and visions to communicate:

The talk they had with the Shining Ones was about the glory of the place, who told them that the beauty and glory of it was inexpressible. There said they, is the Mount Sion, the heavenly Jerusalem, the innumerable company of Angels and the Spirits of just men made perfect. You are going now, said they, to the Paradise of God, wherein you shall see the Tree of Life, and eat of the never-fading fruits thereof; and when you come there, you shall have white Robes given you, and your walk and talk shall be every day with the King, even all the days of Eternity. There you shall not see again such things as you saw when you were in the lower Region upon the earth, to wit, sorrow, sickness, affliction, and death, for the former things are passed away. You are now going to Abraham, Isaac and Jacob, and to the Prophets, men that God hath taken away from the evil to come, and that are now resting upon their beds, each one walking in his righteousness . . . You must there receive the comfort of all your toil, and have joy for all your sorrow; you must reap what you have sown, even the fruit of all your Prayers and Tears, and sufferings for the King by the way. In that place you must wear Crowns of Gold, and enjoy the perpetual sight and vision of the Holy One, for there you shall see him as he is.[1]

Doesn't that lift your spirit and make you want to shout out loud?

NDEs have become increasingly familiar. Dr Raymond Moody, a psychiatrist, was the first individual to start research and began with 150 researched reports. The resultant book sold over 13 million copies. Not proof of veracity, but indicative of the interest. If I had written this book ten years ago, certainly twenty years ago, I would have dismissed the thought of including any serious reference. But my views have changed, and I think it's an area of apologetics that cannot simply be ignored. Most (not all), are consistently descriptive, even when the 'recipient' is not from a religious culture prescribed to certain views or possibilities. Importantly in the context of this book, where such experiences support the scriptural definitions, I believe they can add colour and fire up our own godly imaginations. Jeremiah, writing in a slightly different context, talks about the difference between straw and grain as a way of contrasting dreams and the word of God.[2] And that maybe helpful here. NDEs are like straw (useful in supporting the grain) and what is written in the word of God is the grain. There are reasons to believe that the straw of NDEs can help us harvest the word of God more fully.

There is understandable scepticism, and there is also real concern. So many of these stories appear with light featuring as a central part of the story, and as we have been rightly taught many times over the years, Satan can disguise himself as an angel of light. The counterfeit doesn't negate the real but as with any suspect counterfeit currency we have to hold it in our hands and check the marks; we have to be sure which currency we are holding when it comes to these experiences. It's also worth remembering that biblical accounts (notably Daniel and Revelation) also consistently describe various forms of light in their heavenly descriptions.

The challenge is, we cannot accept every report without care and scrutiny. Some in print have been distinctly un-Christian in their writings and counter to scripture. Others include terrifying stories of life beyond the grave, with torment, darkness and a lake of fire. It's reassuring that for many, these dark experiences have often been a provocation to seek Jesus and make heaven a certain destination. But with all those caveats and with a degree of care, it is worth exploring some of the many thousand stories in print that perhaps, like trip advisor reviews, can be viewed as offering some helpful glimpses of our stopover destination. And, like trip advisor reviews, accept that you cannot ever totally vouch for the accuracy or the source. Equally, like trip advisor reviews, if they all score 4+ for different attributes you can be reasonably certain that's a good approximation of what to expect. We can approach these accounts with both an open mind and a healthy pinch of salt, ensuring that the ones we might take comfort from do concur with scripture – and every NDE should be held up to the light and ultimately measured against scripture.

So, with a couple of exceptions, I have chosen stories for this chapter from people in my church world, who I and other close friends know well and who I can trust. People who haven't written books, people who I heard these stories from for the first time, even though I had known them for years. These are trip advisor reviews from known, reliable sources.

NDEs and Their Place in Our Understanding

A number of books have been written on this subject, but if you are looking for a balanced, carefully researched book, *Imagine Heaven* by John Burke fits that bill well. In his introduction Burke says, 'After reading hundreds of NDE accounts, I started to see the difference between what they *reported* experiencing and the *interpretation* they might give to that experience. While interpretations vary, I found the shared core experience points to what the Scriptures say. In fact, the more I studied, the more I realized that the picture Scripture paints of the exhilarating Life to come is the common experience that NDErs describe.'[3]

Steve Miller notes the quantity of scholarly, peer-reviewed literature now available since Moody wrote *Life After Death*: 'Over 900 articles on NDEs were published in scholarly literature prior to 2011, gracing the pages of such varied journals as *Psychiatry*, *The Lancet*, *Critical Care Quarterly*, *The Journal for Near Death Studies*, *American Journal of Psychiatry*, *British Journal of Psychiatry*, *Resuscitation and Neurology*.'[4]

In a study published in *The Lancet*, van Lommel and colleagues list ten elements of the NDE:[5]

1. Awareness of being dead
2. Positive emotions
3. Out of body experience
4. Moving through a tunnel
5. Communication with light
6. Observation of colours
7. Observation of a celestial landscape
8. Meeting with deceased persons
9. Life review
10. Presence of border

One handbook chronicles that in 65 studies of more than 3,500 NDEs there are common themes, as evidenced above in *The Lancet* journal, and many, although not all, have come to the conclusion that there is life after death as a result.

In this chapter I want to select a couple of outcomes that are common in NDEs and in 'glimpses of heavenly realms' and relate them to some of the truths we have been exploring, so that like the straw they may just help our minds harvest the grain of truth.

A Glimpse of Eternity – Ian McCormack

We had Ian McCormack preaching in Basingstoke some years back. His story is told in his book *A Glimpse of Eternity* and in countless videos on YouTube.[6]

At the time of this story, Ian, in his early twenties, was not a Christian and had very little knowledge of God or scripture. He was stung by a box jellyfish in Mauritius, was transported by ambulance to hospital, where he was pronounced dead and his body transferred to the morgue. In his story, he relates how he began to come out of his body and found himself at first above the hospital, an unnerving sensation he recalls.

He was then startled to find himself in a dark place, so dark he couldn't see his hand in front of his face. While trying to come to terms with this experience, he realized with a shock that his hand had passed through his face. He remembered that just before he had died in the ambulance, he had found himself praying out the Lord's Prayer, and in the only way he knew at the time was aware that he was crying out to God with heartfelt meaning. He realized this experience of darkness was hell, and reflecting afterwards, he felt that this very real experience of darkness and accompanying torment which he was being exposed to, was very likely given to him as an experience of the stark contrast between the hellish torment and darkness and the saving grace which he was about to taste.

Next, Ian describes going upwards into light. Rather like specks of dust rise in the sunlight, he found himself drawn, at what felt like the speed of light, into a narrow passageway of light. Light features dramatically and in many ways in his recounting. He describes waves of light and waves of comfort at these early stages of ascent, with indescribable feelings of love and peace.

This light-infused journey brought him to an encounter with the risen Jesus clothed in garments of indescribable light and he describes how at one point, while he was thinking and not even yet asking questions, answers were coming. He had one particular moment where he felt his childhood innocence restored to his soul. At every stage, he was aware of this light emanating from Jesus reaching for what seemed like infinity without diminishing. He later understood from Revelation 21:23 that 'the city has no need of sun or moon to shine on it, for the glory of God gives it light, and its lamp is the Lamb.'

Peace went through him, and that peace hasn't left him in thirty years since. As with many NDErs, he was aware of differences in his body. His hand and arms were transparent, they looked like hands and arms but also looked like light. The whole place, he says, was a kingdom of such radiance. At one point he was thinking of a question and the answer seemed given in light. And while he was pondering this, words of light appeared, as it were, in the sky above him: 'God is light: in him there is no darkness at all'.

He describes a moment where he went through a door and saw beautiful, verdant green grass, flowers, a crystal-clear river, fields and mountains, similar to and yet at the same time nothing like his native New Zealand. He called it an 'untouched paradise'. This beauty was doubly meaningful for Ian, as an educated agronomist. He remembered thinking that if he stood on that grass it would spring straight back. Much later, he would learn John 10:9, 'I am the door. If anyone enters by me, he will be saved and will go in and out and find pasture.'

In summing up his experience before re-entering his body and giving the mortician a shock, he put it this way: 'Every part of me knows I am home. No one who has been there ever wants to come back.' His journey lasted in planetary time around twenty minutes. Shortly afterwards, he gave his life to Christ and has spent his life sharing his story in a variety of settings around the world, leading others to faith in Jesus.

A Glimpse of Heaven's Welcome –
Chris and Carole Clarke-Williams

Chris and Carole are long standing members of our church and have been faithfully serving God there in a variety of roles for more than two decades.

On a cold Monday evening, Chris drove Carole to Basingstoke Hospital for a planned caesarean delivery, following what had felt like a normal pregnancy. This was their third caesarean and was a familiar path for them both to travel. Chris was there when Shula was born at 10.00 the following morning, Tuesday 6th January.

All looked well at first, but fairly quickly Carole began to sense that things were not right. Shula was not feeding and alarm bells started ringing for Carole. Shula seemed to her to have poor muscle tone and didn't feel like a newborn should. The baby hadn't cried.

Carole shared her concerns with the doctors and nursing staff; they didn't seem too concerned. But it turned out that her fears were well-founded. Coming back to her room after visiting the bathroom, Carole discovered Shula was not there. A nurse came in and rushed her down to special care, where Shula was hooked up to monitors and had multiple blood tests. Shula spent what time was left in special care.

On the night of the 7th, Chris and Carole met with the pastor of their church. They prayed for healing and intentionally committed Shula to God's care. As the night wore on, Chris was asked by the staff to encourage Carole to go back up to her ward and get some rest, which she did.

A few hours later, Dr Walters the lead paediatrician who had come in from a night off to take charge of Shula's care, told Chris that they were seriously worried about Shula's condition and asked if he and Carole wanted to have her baptized. Chris replied that they had already done what was needed.

Chris was then asked to wake Carole up, which he did, and together they sat by Shula's cot until the doctors disconnected the monitors and handed Shula to Carole. She died in Carole's arms.

After Shula died, Chris and Carole were touched by the grief of the team looking after her, and spent some time comforting them and assuring them that they had done all that they could. The worst part for Carole was coming away and leaving her baby at the hospital. 'Leaving hospital without a baby', she writes, 'was a shock. It's something you just don't expect to do. Coming home and telling Deyna, 2, and Ayliffe, 4, was very difficult, while handling your own grief at the same time.' Carole said with feeling: 'If I hadn't been a Christian they would have had to lock me up and keep the key.'

At some point after Shula's funeral, Carole wasn't sure if she was asleep or awake, but she found herself back in time and in the morgue. Shula was in a Moses basket, she had her normal colour and had opened her eyes. There were people standing there as if they were waiting, and then they said, 'Here she comes!'

For Chris and Carole that was a glimpse of Shula's departure and heavenly arrival. It was confirmation that Jesus had taken her. For both Chris and Carole it left them confident and with no doubt as to where she had gone. Chris writes: 'In some ways, we both feel that what happened with Shula was a mercy, although of course we were very much on edge when, subsequently, our two boys were born. We look forward to seeing her when we get to heaven, or at the Resurrection if that happens first.'

A Glimpse of Heaven – Carol Rees

Carol has been a family friend for three decades, and is a member of our church. While I was writing this book, she shared the following story:

Sometime after having my second child, I lost a baby because of an ectopic pregnancy. Troubled and unable to sleep in the hospital, I walked down the passage to the lounge. As I went through the door, God gave me a sudden, breathtaking vision of a young child running into heaven. Through an expanse of soft green grass, gently ruffled by the breath of God, surrounded by the wonderful, perfect light of his loving presence, the child ran with joy.

I sensed God speak, 'His name is John.'

I had questioned the Lord about how I would be able to bear it if I lost one of my children that I loved so much, and I knew in that moment that if I could reach out my hand to him and take him back, I would never, ever do it. The child was completely at home. It was not an unknown place; there was a sense of beginning rather than ending.

Mary and Barrie Wood – an NDE

Part of our Salt & Light church family, Mary tells her story:

We'd recently moved to Oxfordshire. My husband Barrie was training for Baptist church leadership. We had no accommodation, so as a family for a short period we were homeless. Some friends in the church had a house in a small village near Thame. They said to us: 'You have no house but you have some money; we have no money but we have a house.' And for a season, we moved in with them.

I've always been a chronic asthmatic and while staying with them I had a really bad asthma attack. I think it was likely a mixture of the stress of being homeless, caring for two young children, and anxiety over all our belongings in store. Plus in the house where we were staying, there was a hairy dog, not great for an asthma sufferer. It was clear during the attack that I wasn't responding to my usual medication, so my friend called her GP.

By the time the doctor came it was early afternoon. I was struggling to breathe, couldn't walk and the normal inhalers and steroids were not touching the symptoms. The doctor examined me and said, I think we need to give you a quick dose of something and started to give me an injection of aminophylline.

The next thing I knew I was in a bright, wonderful place, everything brighter than bright. I felt an extraordinarily complete peace, an 'at home' feeling. 'Praise the Lord' was glittering in the bright sky and I had an awareness of the presence of Jesus and other people, but I can't recall that I actually saw specific individuals.

The main thing that stood out was that this place was brighter than bright. There was an amazing clarity; everything I looked at was so in focus, nothing was blurry. It was fascinating because it was a long and short distance at the same time. There were lots of people around and I remember wondering if I would see my grandma. There were normal-looking people wandering around in a normal way – no sense of people being abnormal. There were lots of different ages and sizes. They were just there.

There was an overarching awe, and an emotion that I can best express as 'this is the place I was made for, this is the place I am meant to be', and an awareness of the presence of God.

I came to with the doctor performing CPR on me. I'd apparently reacted badly to the injection. It had stopped my heart and I'd died for a very short time – around 10 minutes. I felt so very disappointed to be back. I realized I hadn't had a sense of missing anyone, in fact I knew I was in a 'better place'.

Meanwhile, Barrie had taken our two children out for the day, around 11 a.m., to the Thame Show. He came back with the children and was met by our very pale and anxious friend. His story is amazing to me . . . He entered our bedroom without the kids. I didn't know I looked any different but he said, 'Mary your whole face is shining, I can see the presence of God around you still.' He was aware that I had a 'golden glow' about me, he shared later that it reminded him of when Moses was in the presence of God and his face shone. Mine gradually faded!

I always thought I would miss my husband and my kids if they were left behind. I don't want to go yet because of my family, for their sakes, but I was so in awe of where I was that who I'd left behind was irrelevant. I was so aware of the presence of God, so aware that I wasn't aware of the people I had left behind. I didn't once think about them while I was there. I was just so amazed to be where I was.

It's given us both a real confidence in the gospel – this is what is awaiting me. I've already had a real taste of an amazing sense of peace, joy, contentment and fulfilment – a sense of completion. I can't wait to go back.

Sue Rau's Near Death Experience
Sue's daughter, Robin Worline, has been our friend for more than ten years. We have worked together in a church in Kalida, Ohio. Robin writes Sue's story here as related to her in March 2019:

My family was raised in a little town in Ohio called Hartsburg. My dad worked as a milk deliveryman for Meadow Gold Milk Company, and my mom was a housewife raising five children. Sheri was 6 years old, I (Robin) was 5 years old, and the triplets, Terri, Barry and Perry, were 3½ years old.

One day we came home from shopping for school clothes and found fire trucks surrounding our home, battling a house fire. Lightning had struck, which created embers that smouldered into a fire. The fire caused moderate damage to our home and we kids had to be sent to three different homes while our house was being renovated.

While out delivering milk one day, my dad found an old one-bedroom mobile home that was available. He dragged it home with a tractor and parked it on our property beside our house. Mom was so excited that she would have her family all back together again! An electrical line was connected from my grandparents' garage next door, and Mom went to task cleaning and getting the mobile home ready to move in.

It was a hot summer day, and my bare-footed brothers, sisters, and I, were out on the front lawn playing. Dad was out on his route delivering milk, and Mom was scrubbing the mobile home down. With a wet washcloth and bucket of water in one hand, she reached up with her other hand and grabbed the back-door handle of the mobile home.

Instantly, a surge of electricity entered her body and prevented her from being able to let go of the handle. She screamed as she was being electrocuted, and my little brother Perry ran towards my mom. She screamed for him not to touch her and it was as if an invisible wall went up to deflect him. He got close to her, then made a curve and continued to run away from her towards my grandparents' house.

A carpenter who was installing siding on my grandparents' home, heard my mom's screams and realized she was being electrocuted. He cut the power supply and unplugged the electrical line. As soon as the electrical current stopped, my mom fell to the ground. She was aware of what was going on, but was unable to move or speak. The carpenter carried my mom to my grandparents' house, where he laid her limp body on the couch. While we were waiting for the ambulance to come, I watched my grandmother get a washcloth and try to wipe the grass stains from my mom's bare feet. The ambulance came and took my mom to the hospital where she stayed for nine days as she recovered.

As my mom tells her story of being electrocuted, she also tells of briefly being in the presence of God. She cannot recall for certain when this happened. Whether it was during the few minutes that the electrical current was running through her body or in the ambulance on the way to the hospital.

She says she remembers a dark tunnel . . . going down, down, down. She suddenly stopped in a dark area where she saw a hole in the ground like a crevice or earthquake fault line. She was on the dark side of the crevice, and on the other side of the crevice was the most beautiful and glorious light. To the left side of the light was a silhouette of a person. She did not know who the person was, but knew it was someone she had a deep love for. This person called her by her nickname 'Susie', and Mom was amazed that this person would know that.

My mom and this person had a conversation. She cannot remember all of it, but does remember telling him that she wanted to cross over the crevice to the beautiful light where he was. She told him the stress of raising the triplets . . . the burden of repairing a burned home . . . and now the painful electrocution . . . was all she could handle. She just couldn't take any more. She wanted to be where he was. The person said, 'No Susie. You cannot cross over to me. You have to go back. You have work to do.' My mom said that more took place during that encounter but cannot recall specifics of what it was. She also does not remember what happened after that, or when she re-entered her body. But she truly feels that the person she saw silhouetted in the glorious light who she'd had a conversation with was God.

She also notes, 'God kept the rest of the details from me. Like in real life. He doesn't show us the whole picture.'

An interesting side note from my mom's experience: for several years after the electrocution, my mom was unable to wear a wristwatch. They could not keep accurate time or would stop altogether.

Father-in-Law Makes Certain

Doug and Nancy Schwartz are friends from Michigan, founders of Firm Foundation Ministries. Doug wrote the following:

My father-in-law Ron had a near death experience after cancer surgery in 1998. In between heartbeats, he was in heaven. He said he saw Jesus in front of him with his arm outstretched pointing at him and said, 'We don't need you up here yet.' And then he was back in his body in the hospital room where my wife Nancy was visiting.

His breathing stabilized and all his vitals stabilized. He asked for me in the waiting room. So, together with the rest of the family, I came in expecting to hear his last dying breath. However, as I got up close, I noticed his eyes were unusually large. He took my hand and said something that was muffled under his oxygen mask. After a few times Nancy said, 'You saw the Lord?' I repeated it and he nodded, saying 'yes' with his eyes still large.

I said, 'Was it peaceful?' And he said a big 'yes' and then he said, 'What do I do now?' I told him to let the doctors and nurses take care of him and get some rest. Expecting his imminent death, I had been praying that God would give us a sign that he had gone to heaven. I just didn't expect him to go there and come back to tell us about it!

The next day we visited him in hospital, and had the opportunity to ask him what he saw. He said that in an instant he was in the most glorious throne room that he had ever seen. There were people all around, but he didn't recognize any of them. Jesus was standing in front of him with his finger pointed and his eyes were so full of love. He said there was a throne behind Jesus with someone sitting on the throne. I asked what colour the throne was and he said it was a chrome colour. He said Jesus didn't even have to speak because he knew his thoughts. When he got 'sent back', he said he felt like the third man on a garbage truck because they were not needed either.

When he came home, and Nancy and I thought we would take him on tour to tell his story over and over, but that didn't happen as his health continued to deteriorate. He lived for six more months, telling his story as people visited him at home. He told Nancy when she visited, stories of his childhood that he had never shared before. This was significant because it was the NDE, the experience, the taste of heaven that had unlocked his emotions. He said to her one day, 'Nancy with everything that God has to take care of in the universe, I can't believe he sent Jesus to tell me that they didn't need me up there yet. He also said that he didn't want to disappoint Jesus.

On Easter Sunday, after most of the family had gone home, I was there with Nancy and our youngest son Seth, together with Nancy's mom. Ron slowly went to sleep. He wanted to stay here. But Nancy's brother said, 'It's okay dad, you can go,' and he immediately took his last breath to be with Jesus. He was scared to die the first time but, amazingly, he knew what peace there was in heaven, so was unafraid this second time.

Nancy and I have shared this story since then many, many times. Especially with people who are dying, to give them hope. If I could add a story of an eyewitness of Jesus to the Bible, I would add this story. What a glorious experience this was. We look forward to seeing him again someday, along with our stillborn son Jonathan.

Revd Ali Kay and a Parishioner

Ali Kay is a long-standing friend, and for years was part of our family of churches. I was indirectly, in a very small way, part of his transition to the Anglican Church, where he currently serves as Priest in Charge of St Francis of Assisi, Mackworth. He wrote the following:

I recently had a quite amazing experience while administering last rites to a lady. In the last three years, half of my congregation have died, and in virtually all cases, I have been there at their death. In this case, suddenly this lady threw her arms in the air and began to talk with my congregation members, who it was clear she could see in heaven. Her final words were, 'I'm coming'. Her family were stunned – and with that, she passed into the presence of God.

An NDE Conversion and a remarkable resurrection

Over thirty years ago I met a remarkable man called John Babu in Hyderabad, India. I later spoke at his church and taught at his Bible college, which close friends from Basingstoke, John and Marilyn Denning, were running for him.

John was in the police force, a senior security advisor to Indira Gandhi, the Prime Minister of India. He was a man of great power and prestige in his home state of Andhra Pradesh. But his life otherwise was a mess. He was an alcoholic, who beat his wife and children nearly every day. He became ill, and received the diagnosis that his liver was failing and he had only a few months to live.

John was a Hindu, though not an observant one, and on hearing the prognosis, he went to his temple and sat inside it weeping. At that moment, he began to hear a voice speaking to him. The voice said very clearly, 'I am the God you are searching for. My name is Jesus Christ. Leave this place and I will show you the way of salvation.' Utterly terrified, he fled the temple and collapsed onto a bench outside. The voice then resumed. It told him that the fate awaiting him was unthinkable, and as the voice spoke, he saw before him a vision of a lake of fire. But it then assured him that he could be saved from this fate if he entrusted his life to the true and living God and to Jesus, his Son. And so he did.

Years later, his eldest son told a friend of mine, David Campbell, of the day he came home from that encounter. He remembered it well because it was the first day his father ever came home without beating him or his mother. And he never did so again. John discovered that his liver was completely healed. He left the police force and devoted himself to planting churches – hundreds of them, in fact. One story he told David stands out.

John had sent a young man out to plant a church in a village. A lady of high caste in the village had died. The priests had cast omens for the most propitious moment for her cremation, so as to ensure the best possible reincarnation. As her body was laid on the pyre, the priest, seeing a golden opportunity to discredit the efforts of the church planter, told the crowd these Christians claimed to have a God who could raise the dead. He ordered the young man to be brought, and when he arrived, he told him to pray for the woman to be brought back to life, just to see what his 'God' could do. The young man in desperation raised his hands over the body laid out on the pyre and called on the name of Jesus.

To the consternation of the gathered crowd of hundreds of people, she was resurrected from the dead. Half of them fled in terror and the other half stayed to hear what I can only say must have been a terrific preaching opportunity.

What was most remarkable was the story the woman later told. She sensed herself in complete darkness, when a figure dressed in brilliant white clothing appeared with his hands raised over her. The man had wounds in both of his wrists. Then she awoke, and she saw a second man, dressed in ordinary clothes and with no wounds in his hands, yet he was standing in the same position with his hands outstretched over her. The woman's testimony had such power in the area that the authorities eventually had her arrested. She told them they could kill her if they wanted. She had already died once and had no fear of dying again.

The same power that raised Jesus from the dead is at work in us who stand in his place, offering life to a dying world.

Captain Dale Black

Captain Dale Black was an airline pilot with over 17,000 hours' flying experience. One fateful day Dale, with two other pilots, took off in a twin engine Piper Navajo and on a faulty take-off veered the plane into a 75-foot-high monument. The plane disintegrated as the three pilots plunged 75 feet to the ground. Only Dale survived. Sort of. Let me share some extracts:

Suddenly I found myself suspended in midair, hovering over the wreckage of my body. My gray pants and short-sleeve shirt were torn to shreds and soaked in blood and fuel . . . I sped through what appeared to be a narrow pathway . . . It wasn't a tunnel of light that I was traveling through. It was a path in the darkness that was delineated by the light. Outside of this pathway was total darkness. But in the darkness millions of tiny spheres of light zoomed past as I traveled through what looked like deep space, almost as if a jet were flying through a snowstorm at night . . . At this time I became aware I was not flying alone. Accompanying me were two angelic escorts dressed in seamless white garments woven with silver threads . . . Remarkably, my peripheral vision was enhanced, and I could see both of their glowing faces at the same time. I could even see behind me while hardly moving my head . . .

The light I saw was the purest I had ever seen. And the music was the most majestic, enchanting, and glorious I had ever heard . . .

I was overwhelmed by its beauty. It was breathtaking. And a strong sense of belonging filled my heart; I never wanted to leave. Somehow, I knew I was made for this place, and this place was made for me . . .

The light was palpable. It had substance to it, weight and thickness, like nothing I had ever seen before or since . . .

Somehow, I knew that light and love were connected and interrelated . . . Remarkably, the light didn't shine on things but through them. Through the grass. Through the trees. Through the wall. And through the people who were gathered there. There was a huge gathering of angels and people, millions, countless millions . . .

I was outside the city, slowly moving toward its wall, suspended a few hundred feet above the ground. I'm not sure how I knew directions there . . . I moved effortlessly along the road, escorted by my two angelic guides . . .

Below me lay the purest, most perfect grass, precisely the right length and not a blade that was bent or even out of place. It was the most vibrant green I had ever seen. If a color can be said to be alive, the green I saw was alive, slightly transparent and emitting light and life from within each blade. The iridescent grass stretched endlessly over gently rolling hills upon which were sprinkled the most colorful wild flowers, lifting their soft-petaled beauty skyward, almost as if they were a chorus of flowers caught up in their own way of praising God.

The fragrance that permeated heaven was so gentle and sweet, I almost didn't notice it amid all there was to see and hear. But as I looked at the delicate, perfect flowers and grass, I wanted to smell them. Instantly, I was aware of a gentle aroma. As I focused, I could tell the difference between the grass and the flowers, the trees and even the air. It was all so pure and intoxicating and blended together in a sweet and satisfying scent.

In the distance stood a range of mountains, majestic in appearance, as if they reigned over the entire landscape. These were not mountains you wanted to conquer; these were mountains you wanted to revere . . .

[The city wall] stretched out to my left and right as far as I could see in both directions . . . A powerful light permeated the wall, and you could see all the colors of the rainbow in it. Strangely, whenever I moved, the colors moved ever so slightly as if sensing my movement and making an adjustment . . .

The grass, the sky, the walls, the houses, everything was more beautiful than I had ever dreamed anything could be. Even the colors. They were richer, deeper, more luminescent than any colors I have ever seen in the farthest reaches of the earth or in the most fantastic of dreams.[7]

It is surely the case that heaven, by everything we know of God and his attributes, by everything we know from scripture, must be more: more beautiful, more colourful, more amazing, more diverse, more creative and all of that without the decay the damage and the destruction of sin. Heaven must be more. Believe it, it's true, believe it because your heart believes it, believe it because of all you know of God, believe it because of every scriptural fragment we have rehearsed in this book.

In Isaiah we are told the angels are calling to one another: 'Holy, holy, holy is the Lord Almighty: the whole earth is full of his glory.' Why then could we ever allow ourselves to think that heaven, where the creator lives in a place he has created, would be less glorious, less beautiful, less magnificent, less colourful?

One other short extract from Ian McCormack's story:

Through the centre of the meadows I could see a crystal-clear stream winding its way across the landscape with trees on either bank. To my right were mountains in the distance and the sky above was blue and clear. To my left were rolling hills and flowers, which were radiating beautiful colours. Paradise! I knew I belonged here. I felt as though I had just been born for the first time. Every part of me knew I was home.[8]

Interesting isn't it how NDErs describe their experience as 'home'. Little wonder, though, when we recall again that Jesus said, 'I go to prepare a place for you.' It's his perfect place for you and me. That's home!

CHAPTER 8

Paradise at Work

———·———

One of the big questions, and I have been asked this countless times, is, 'What do we do in heaven?' Behind the question lies some of the fears we explored in Chapter 3, and in particular the stereotyped view of heaven as a place of rest and endless Sunday services. It's also one of the reasons why passion seems to run so low for preaching about, speaking about and dialoguing about heaven. In a generation epitomised by its advancements in technology, science and workplace meaning, heaven as an eternal fly and flop destination has no appeal.

It's interesting too that at first glance there is apparently little laid out line by line in scripture, but actually, with open minds and open eyes we can quickly discern a whole raft of clues.

A Daily Prayer with Heavenly Implications

The most famous of all prayers ever written, prayed probably millions of times every day around the world is the so-called

'Lord's Prayer'. Recorded for us in Matthew and Luke. Matthew tells us:

Pray then like this:

'Our Father in heaven,
hallowed be your name.
Your kingdom come,
your will be done,
on earth as it is in heaven.'[1]

What we see here is quite remarkable. We are reminding ourselves daily that our Father is from heaven – that's his address. We are reminding ourselves daily that his heavenly kingdom is to be prayed for, to be reached for, to be extended on earth. We are reminding ourselves daily that earth is not the reality and heaven somehow a shadow or reflection, rather it is heaven that is the reality and earth that is the reflection. We are reminding ourselves daily that in heaven there is activity, action and function – his will is being done. We are reminding ourselves daily that as the will of God is being done in heaven, we should long for, ask for, that same planned and purposeful activity to be expressed in our lives on earth. Earth is not the reality with heaven somehow a second best. Heaven is all that we were ever designed to be and enjoy. Heaven is the reality, earth is the shadow.

Heaven is not the resting place after I have done God's work on earth. Heaven is not a disengaged holiday destination where I sit by the pool play Christian music and contemplate. Heaven is the hub, the command centre, the operational base from which kingdom sorties on earth are directed, resourced and planned. Whatever we do on earth can only be a reflection of what the king of heaven is purposing, directing, planning, resourcing.

Jesus did the work of the father in a very different way to our prevailing view of service for God. The gospels record him once only singing a single hymn. He did very little kingdom work in the church building. He travelled with his disciples, trained them and commissioned them into jobs and roles that stretched their capacity and their competence. He ate and drank with them, prepared feasts and barbeques. Yes, synagogue appears in the gospels 68 times, but mostly in reference to the religious. In contrast, lake appears 35 times, boat 42, hill 7, garden 5, mount 11, sea 15, villages 27, shore 10, house 89. That is 241:68 or 3.5:1. You get the point, I'm sure. This is the same Jesus who prayed every day, 'Your kingdom come, your will be done on earth as it is in heaven. Putting it another way, this is one reflection of what God's will looks like in heaven and on earth. Eden was always intended to be a place where God and man lived and worked together, and work as service to God and for God was integral to that notion. This way of working, this manner of service, led to the twelve apostles having the honour of having their names on twelve foundations on the wall of the city of the new Jerusalem. That's high praise indeed!

In John's gospel Jesus says, 'My Father is always at his work to this very day'.[2] In other words making it clear that this same Father in heaven has not stopped working since creation. He is still sustaining, directing, intervening with his creation. In the same verse, Jesus goes on to declare that in the same way his father was working in heaven, he was working on earth. On earth as it is in heaven.

There is a famous scripture read every year during carol services around the world. The implications are wonderful. Speaking of the Messiah, Isaiah says: 'Of the increase of his government . . . there will be no end'.[3] Read it again: 'Of the increase of his government . . . there will be no end'. It's not just that his government, his place of rule is eternal and heavenly, but more powerfully it is eternally increasing. Fly and flop is not increase, it's passive rest. Rest and worship is mostly passive, wonderful for a time maybe. But we are talking about a kingdom that is unstoppably increasing, growing, expanding. Think about this, shout it out with a 'Hallelujah!' if you want. That needs a plan, that needs resource, that needs people and that needs supernatural beings, because we know from elsewhere in scripture that's exactly how God outworks his will.

The kingdom of heaven, mentioned 31 times in the gospels, is never presented as passive. It's like a small seed that grows into a big shrub, so the birds of the air nest. It's represented by the parable of the sower, where a harvest is expected thirty-, sixty- and a hundred-fold. It's like the process of leaven which spreads into the whole dough. Increase on earth as it is in heaven. The essential element seems to be, seed germinates and grows, yeast keeps growing, and that's active increase out of all proportion to its small beginnings.

From the very first pages of scripture in his very first Eden garden paradise, God is seen by name, by nature and by evidence, as designer, creator and ruler. God is, by nature, a God of increase. In the first three chapters of Genesis alone, God is recorded as one who makes, forms, plants and builds. That doesn't stop at death for us, and most certainly doesn't stop with the King of heaven. In scripture, most of the rewards that are promised us in heaven are rewards that have to do with increase, and with responsibility. That's our reward. Know then for a certainty, positive, productive, fruitful, practical service for God is the way it is in heaven. On earth . . . as it is in heaven. Oh wonderful, worshipful working partnership with our Father in heaven.

First, Front and Centre

The same scripture we read in Isaiah that talks of the increase of his government, also shows us what is first and foremost in that increase.

Of the increase of his government and of peace
    there will be no end,
on *the throne* of David and over his kingdom,
    to establish it and to uphold it
with justice and with righteousness

from this time forth and for evermore.
The zeal of the LORD of hosts will do this.[4]

The command hub of the cosmic purposes of God is his throne. We see this in Isaiah, Ezekiel, Daniel, Psalms, Stephen's stoning and in Revelation. In Appendix II I have extended the following passages, because the beauty of what was seen is breathtaking. But enough to put in place here the importance of what is fundamental in visions of heaven in both the Old and New Testaments:

Isaiah
In the year that King Uzziah died I saw the Lord sitting upon *a throne*, high and lifted up; and the train of his robe filled the temple.[5]

Ezekiel
And above the expanse over their heads there was the likeness of a throne, in appearance like sapphire; and seated above the likeness of *a throne* was a likeness with a human appearance.[6]

Daniel
As I looked,

> thrones were placed,
> and the Ancient of Days took his seat;
> his clothing was white as snow,
> and the hair of his head like pure wool;
> *his throne* was fiery flames;

its wheels were burning fire.
A stream of fire issued
and came out from before him;
a thousand thousands served him,
and ten thousand times ten thousand stood before him;[7]

Psalms
The Lord has established *his throne* in the heavens,
and his kingdom rules over all.[8]

Revelation
After this I looked, and behold, a door standing open in heaven! And the first voice, which I had heard speaking to me like a trumpet, said, 'Come up here, and I will show you what must take place after this.' At once I was in the Spirit, and behold, *a throne* stood in heaven, with one seated on the throne.[9]

Stephen, in his last seconds on earth and just before his first seconds in paradise, quotes from the Old Testament in his closing words, saying, 'Heaven is *my throne*, and the earth is my footstool.'[10]

In other words, in paradise the throne is first, front and centre. The centrality of the throne and the Lamb gives us a clue, and it demonstrates that the whole of heaven reflects the ongoing work of God, started in Eden, redeemed at Calvary and which, like seed and yeast, is increasing forever. It makes it clear that it is an eternally growing work. The central feature in heavenly images and metaphors in scripture is a throne. A throne is not a motif of passivity and rest. All heaven revolves around this throne. This is a heaven filled with rule, reign and purpose. The throne of God and of the Lamb is not just an icon, a motif to focus our sung worship, it's the centre point of increase, the centre point of function, the centre point of future growth. All the angelic and heavenly creatures recorded in places such as Daniel, Ezekiel, Isaiah and John in Revelation have this everlasting throne as their focal point.

And where this throne is recorded it's always accompanied by activity, movement, mobility and, by inference, 'a thousand thousand' serving him. The King of heaven issuing commands on the basis of a plan, and all his servants engaged in the practical outworking of that plan. That plan is working out on earth as well as heaven. Angels in heaven rejoice over one sinner that repents. Why? Because the plan of heaven includes the work of God on earth – 'On earth as it is in heaven'. In Hebrews we are told of the great cloud of witnesses that surround us. These are heroes of the faith now in heaven who are watching the contest, the race that is being run. Whatever their role, the point is made again: heaven and earth are connected, so much so that we are encouraged in that verse, because of these witnesses in heaven, to throw off everything that hinders us and run with perseverance the race marked out for us.[11]

A throne implies ruling over an expanding kingdom. All heaven revolves around this throne and the Lamb is at the centre of that throne. His loving care for his own in the place he prepared for them at the moment he died for them, yes. But it's far more than that. This is not a temporary throne, this is a throne at the heart of increase, increase of government, increase of peace, and of that increase there will be no end. No end to increase. This is not a throne in front of the choir stalls and the orchestra. This is a throne that issues commands, and angels on horseback with swords respond. This is a throne with books and records and campaign plans, and legions of angels that together with the people of God respond.

Work in Heaven

God's throne is mentioned more than 40 times in Revelation alone. Some references are in present heaven and some in the new heaven and new earth. That throne is not a figure of speech, it's a description of reality. God is ruling, and ruling over growth, extension and increase. It's interesting too that work, or function and service are seen as rewards. We pick this up more fully in Chapter 10. Even those who come out of the great tribulation will be especially rewarded by being given a place 'before the throne of God', where they will serve him day and night. The word 'serve' in this context can mean a number of things, but its root is in the work of a hired hand.

In some Christian circles there is a notion (albeit diminishing) that work and service are somehow secondary to contemplation. It was Marian Wright Edelman who put it this way, 'Service is the rent we pay for being. It is the very purpose of life'.[12] So yes of course the environment in present heaven (our place of stopover) and in the new heaven and new earth will be different. But the nature of who we were created to be doesn't change. In fellowship with God, in partnership with God, we will be serving and worshipping with our voices, whatever they might sound like, and with our very beings.

In Daniel, we see earthly kingdoms giving way to an ultimate eternal kingdom ruled over by the saints: 'The saints of the Most High shall receive the kingdom and possess the kingdom for ever, for ever and ever.'[13] Surely that is service, and that service is work. The same passage goes on to say 'a thousand thousands served him, and ten thousand times ten thousand stood before him'. The Hebrew word for served here has 'activity' in mind, and is potentially linked with a little-used word that implies 'to be brilliant'.[14]

My suggestion here is simple: rest is not the goal of heaven. There is rest in heaven and I'm sure it's wonderful, but it is in the context of service and work. Lots of Christians know the scripture in Hebrews about entering rest,[15] and Revelation tells us, 'Blessed are the dead who die in the Lord from now on. Blessed indeed, says the Spirit, that they will rest from their labours, for their deeds follow them!'[16] So rest features in paradise, as it did in Eden. It follows too that pre-curse unspoilt service and work will feature in paradise, as it was designed, purposed and intended to in the pre-curse Eden.

Work is not the result of the fall. Work was there before the fall. Part of God's personality and integral to his faultless design. Work is beautiful it is good it is one of God's outstanding diamonds in the crown of creation. Work was to be part of Adam's richest fellowship with his maker. And yes, the fall tainted work, and brought thorns to the rose bush and weeds to the flower displays. But the rose and the flowerbed were there before and are still there now. Men and women together from the very beginning were created to have fellowship with each other and with God by working on his planet. Serving each other and serving God in the process. It is worth asking the question: Where did Adam have his intimate time with God? In the garden. What was that? His place of work; the setting for the work that God had given him to do.

There is glory in our work. God made us in his image so that we can fulfil his purpose in ourselves and in the world by working.

As we have seen, we read that in paradise and in the new heavens and new earth too, the throne of God and of the Lamb will be in the city, and his servants will serve him. 'Serve' is a working word, a function word, a doing word, a verb. The resurrected Jesus was still working on the plans and purposes of his father, moving, travelling, preparing, feeding, eating, connecting. Colossians reminds us: 'Whatever you do, work at it with all your heart, as working for the Lord, not human masters, since you know that you will receive an inheritance from the Lord as a reward. It is the Lord Christ you are serving.'[17]

'Throughout eternity, we will live full, truly human lives, exploring and managing God's creation to his glory. Fascinating vistas will unfold before us as we learn to serve God in a renewed universe,' says Edward Donnelly.[18] Victor Hugo clearly anticipated something similar, as towards the end of his life he wrote the following:

I feel within me that future life. I am like a forest that has been razed; the new shoots are stronger and brighter. I shall most certainly rise toward the heavens . . . The nearer my approach to the end, the plainer is the sound of immortal symphonies of worlds which invite me. For half a century I have been translating my thoughts into prose and verse: history, philosophy, drama, romance, tradition, satire, ode and song; all of these I have tried. But I feel I haven't given utterance to the thousandth part of what lies within me. When I go to the grave I can say, as others have said, 'My day's work is done.' But I cannot say, 'My life is done.' My work will recommence the next morning. The tomb is not a blind alley; it is a thoroughfare. It closes upon the twilight, but opens upon the dawn.[19]

This deeply impacts those of us who have lost a son, a daughter, a brother, a sister, a husband or wife in the prime of life. When fantastic dreams and godly aspirations lie buried in the body of the one we loved so much, it is likely that a heart-wrenching thought will come crashing with tsunami-like force, 'what a waste'.

However, if we believe as we do that of the increase of his government there will be no end, and if we believe that the parable of the talents implies that what we have put to work here is in fact proving preparation for even more creative responsibility to come, we can set our minds at rest. If we believe that in all things (even the apparently untimely death of a loved one) God works together for good for those who love him, do we seriously think that is for this life only? No, it cannot be. The inference from the scriptures that talk about reward for work begun in this life, tip heavily like weighed scales towards the reality that that reward is further service in the life to come.

The New Testament tells us:[20]

- We shall reign with him
- We shall rule and judge angels
- We shall have authority over cities
- We shall have authority over nations

You can't do these things without work, service, function Increase.

Think for a moment about the scale of the new city, the heavenly Jerusalem. We are told that the measurements are 'man's measurements' and this city is larger than anything ever seen on earth to date. It's an architectural wonder. Apparently a cube, it is 1,200 stadia in length, breadth and height – that's 1,400 miles long, wide and high. Think of France for example, which is 246,000 square miles. The whole of Europe is said to equal 1.55 million square miles. Compare that to the new Jerusalem at 1.96 million square miles. Imagine the design ingredients, imagine the construction elements, imagine the architectural wonders to be unpacked. The future is bright: it is heart-stoppingly, jaw-droppingly, wonderfully, creatively bright. It's big, it's growing, and all of heaven's inhabitants – human beings and heavenly creatures (angels, archangels, seraphim and cherubim) – are actively serving the purposes of the one on the throne.

If the kingdom of God is eternally expanding, increasing, progressing, then there will always be learning. Ephesians suggest that in the coming ages he will show or reveal the incomparable riches of his grace. The entire verse implies ongoing age-to-age progressive revelation. The fact that our ultimate destination is a new heaven and a new earth implies a whole host of new things that will stimulate and necessitate learning.

The word serve and servant(s) appear sixteen times in Revelation, enough to imply there is service to be done. David Gregg says, 'It is work as free from care and toil and fatigue as is the wing-stroke of the jubilant lark when it soars into the sunlight of a fresh, clear day and, spontaneously and for self-relief, pours out its thrilling carol. Work 'up there' is a matter of self-relief, as well as a matter of obedience to the ruling will of God. It is work according to one's tastes and delight and ability. If tastes vary there, if abilities vary there, then occupations will vary there.'[21]

'His servants will worship him. They will see his face'.[22] 'We are, says Maclaren, saplings here but we shall be transported into our heavenly soil to grow in God's light. Here our abilities are in blossom; there they shall burst forth with fruits of greater beauty. Our death is but the passing from one degree of loving service to another . . . Our love for God will continue, but awakened with new purity and purposefulness.'[23]

CHAPTER 9

Angels in Paradise

———

It's interesting that in the same way that contemporary phrases almost trivialise the word 'heaven', something similar happens with the word 'angel'. Some time back, I was violently sick and thought I might be having some form of heart attack. My paramedic daughter Cheryl-Ann turned up. She was instantly in charge. Her loving hands held the bowl when others would have found that just too much. And, immediately, with her confident competence I felt at peace. She cut through NHS bureaucracy and got me sorted efficiently.

When I texted her later to thank her, I talked about her being a gift from God in her person and in her professional skill, but actually as a person carrying and operating in a God-given gift. I said to her, without even thinking about it, that 'I felt touched by heaven'. I reflected later that at the time it was like having an angelic visit and then found myself reflecting also on common usage of that term. We say superficially, 'Oh she's angelic', or when someone helps us in a crisis in an extraordinarily loving or effective way we say 'What an angel!'

Somewhere deep within our beings we instinctively seem to know that angels are agents of God on earth to help handle the toughest of times. We even see this exemplified with Jesus in gethsemane.

Little wonder then that we discover angels are big to God, big in scripture and very big in present heaven. Jesus told the disciples they would see heaven opened and angels ascending and descending on the Son of man. Of 284 references in scripture to angel(s), 77 of those references are in the book of Revelation – that's 27 per cent. That's a clear focus, a paradise focus. And as we saw in Chapter 8, the blend of angelic activity includes worship and consistent, continuous, mission-critical activity. Consistent intentional, strategic service, outworking the purposes of God in heaven and on earth. Wherever you look, angels are seen as messengers, agents of the kingdom of heaven, committed to seeing the prayer of Jesus answered, committed to seeing the will of God done on earth as it is in heaven. Angels operate on earth as they also operate in heaven. Angels are a reminder of the link, the proximity between earth and heaven. Angels help to ensure that the will of God in heaven is carried out as they facilitate and serve us here on earth.

One of my favourite hotels in the UK is Luton Hoo. It's a fabulous place, with history that involves the Russian aristocracy. Winston Churchill spoke from its balconies and British tanks were seen there in WW 2. Some of Churchill's original paintings are displayed on the walls. But the place I love most is the restaurant at breakfast time. Great food, as you would expect, with sweeping views down to a private lake. But the main reason I love this room is an ancient tapestry on the wall depicting various periods of English history. It's big, you can't ignore it. It's approximately 2 metres high and 6 metres long; each individual section is stand-alone, but together the whole piece provides a narrative, a story.

Looking at an overview of angelic appearances and intervention in scripture is similar, in the sense that each story is stand-alone, but stitched together, a picture emerges and a narrative. That overarching story and the individual threads remind us of the connection between present heaven and earth, and the place of angels in both.

If I asked you to guess what the first mention of angels was in the Bible, I wonder what you would guess. You could argue that it was the cherubim with a flaming sword placed to prevent anyone entering the garden of Eden and eating the tree of life. But the cherubim are another species of heavenly being, not angels. The first direct reference to an angel is a heart-warming response to a female slave called Hagar. In a chilling story, Hagar is a surrogate mother for Abraham and Sarai. Sarai mistreats her and she runs away. Four times an angel speaks to her telling her to return and submit to her mistress, and then prophecies over her son to be called Ishmael.[1] She returns, and the story has another twist worthy of a soap opera. She is sent away by Abraham with some bread and water. When the water runs out, she puts Ishmael under a bush and weeps. The angel of God calls to Hagar and opens her eyes to a source of water.[2]

Two angels are involved in attempting to get Lot and his family out of Sodom and Gomorrah, and manage to persuade Lot, his wife and his daughters to move out. Presumably, they were in some way involved with the sulphur and fire that were then sent upon Sodom and Gomorrah from heaven.[3]

The angel of the Lord calls from heaven and stops Abraham sacrificing Isaac, and in the same passage goes on to reaffirm the covenant of God with Abraham and his descendants.[4]

Abraham's servant was aware of an angel helping him prosper in the process of finding a wife for Isaac.[5]

While working for Laban, Jacob met an angel in a dream who gave him a genetic strategy for selecting the best goats. Jacob leaves Laban, his father-in-law, taking his wives and Laban's grandchildren with him. As Jacob went on his way, the angels of God met him. 'And he dreamed, and behold, there was a ladder set up on the earth, and the top of it reached to heaven. And behold, the angels of God were ascending and descending on it!' He saw angels ascending and descending in his stairway to heaven! God spoke to him from above the opening to heaven and reaffirmed the covenant given to Abraham. When he woke early in the morning Jacob said, 'This is none other than the house of God, and this is the gate of heaven.'[6] An angel in the form of a man wrestled with Jacob all night, just prior to him meeting his estranged brother Esau. The angel eventually puts Jacob's leg out of socket and fundamentally weakens Jacob's natural strength.[7]

An angel was designated to lead the children of Israel through the wilderness.[8]

The angel of the Lord greets Gideon, and with the tip of his staff barbeques the meat, some cakes and a broth, and then vanishes from Gideon's sight. That experience gave Gideon Jehovah Shalom God's peace for the upcoming battles.[9]

The angel of the Lord appeared to Manoah and his wife promised them a child which was to be Samson. 'And when the flame went up toward heaven from the altar, the angel of the LORD went up in the flame of the altar. Now Manoah and his wife were watching, and they fell on their faces to the ground.'[10]

Daniel describes interaction three times with the angel Gabriel who is told to 'make this man understand the vision'. Gabriel came to Daniel in swift flight. Daniel also meets Michael who is described as one of the chief princes who has charge of the people of Israel. [11]

Jesus more than anyone else in scripture engages with angels and clarifies their role, function and purpose. An angel (Gabriel) appears to Zechariah to announce the impending arrival of John the Baptist as the son of Zechariah and Elizabeth. The same angel is sent to Mary to announce the favour of God and answering her question describes to her how the messiah to be named Jesus would be born through her.[12] An angel appears to Joseph in a dream and explains the nature of Mary's conception.[13] At the birth of Jesus, an angel announces the good news to the shepherds and then a multitude of the heavenly host declare glory to God and peace on earth. Subsequently, an angel appears to Joseph twice and gives Joseph travel instructions to ensure the baby Jesus goes first to Egypt and then to Nazareth thus fulfilling ancient prophecies in the process.[14]

Angels come and minister to Jesus after his temptation in the wilderness.[15] He describes angels as the reapers at the end of the age they are tasked to gather and separate at the harvest at the end of the age.[16] Jesus prophesies his own return and tells us that the Son of Man is going to come with his angels in the glory of his father and 'he will send out his angels with a loud trumpet call, and they will gather his elect from the four winds, from one end of heaven to the other.[17] He has twelve legions of angels that he can call on. Nathanael is told that he will 'see heaven opened, and the angels of God ascending and descending on the Son of Man.'[18]

We are told by Jesus that angels carried Lazarus to heaven.[19] We are carefully instructed, 'See that you do not despise one of these little ones. For I tell you that in heaven their angels always see the face of my Father who is in heaven.'[20]

Jesus goes on to tell us that when we rise from the dead we will be like the angels in heaven, neither married nor given in marriage.[21] We cannot die any more because we are 'equal to angels and are sons of God, being sons of the resurrection.'[22]

When Jesus rose from the dead, 'an angel of the Lord descended from heaven and came and rolled back the stone and sat on it.'[23] Two angels in white deal with the grief-stricken Mary Magdalene when she visits the now empty tomb, enabling her to see the risen Jesus.[24]

When Jesus ascends into heaven, two angels in white robes explain, 'Jesus, who was taken up from you into heaven, will come in the same way as you saw him go into heaven.'[25]

An angel frees the apostle Peter from prison,[26] appears to Philip telling him to go and meet the Ethiopian eunuch and changes the course of world history, as well as the salvation of one man.[27] An angel appears to Cornelius and, from that encounter, the apostle Peter preaches to the gentiles.[28] An angel strikes down Herod[29] and makes Paul understand that he must stand before Caesar.[30]

Peter tells us Jesus 'has gone into heaven and is at the right hand of God, with angels, authorities, and powers having been subjected to him.'[31] In Revelation we discover that churches have angels,[32] and we see angels in a myriad of activities. 'And I saw a strong angel proclaiming with a loud voice, "Who is worthy to open the scroll and break its seals?"'[33] Another angel gathers the prayers of the saints and offers incense with those prayers.[34] Seven angels sound trumpets and all kinds of disastrous activity takes place on earth. The angels are despatched with specific messages. Angels pour bowls that in turn produce sores, contaminate sea and rivers, change the power of the sun to scorch the earth, darkness falls and the river Euphrates dries up. An angel throws a millstone into the sea.[35] John is told by angels what and when to write.

This is a tapestry of individual strands making up identifiable pictures and forming an overall narrative. Angels do worship, but the references to angels worshipping in song are few. Let me bullet-point just some of the things that angels based in the command centre, the strategic hub, the throne room of paradise do:

- give direction
- ascend and descend
- bring illumination
- bring judgement
- help individuals
- look over children – children's angels constantly behold the face of the father in heaven implying constant activity on behalf of little ones
- look over churches
- look over nations
- look over geographical territories
- Michael is called an archangel in Jude and is a warrior
- angels go up in flames to heaven
- they speak with humans both on earth and in heaven
- they can fly swiftly
- they don't marry
- they are intimately involved in carrying out the commands of God now and in the unfolding end times
- they rejoice with us in heaven over sinners turning to Christ
- they appear as ordinary people
- they also appear in white clothing
- they are often not recognized unless they choose to reveal themselves

- they are all ministering spirits sent to serve for the sake of those who are to inherit salvation
- we are told on earth to entertain strangers because some of us will be entertaining angels unawares
- they are often involved – sometimes we know and see and sometimes we don't
- they know our names
- they are co-labourers, fellow servants
- Gabriel is named in scripture, not specifically as an archangel but clearly senior with special roles
- carry those who die to paradise
- change and intervene in history

All through scripture, people believed in angels and believed explicitly that they were involved in the events of earth. They were perceived to be fighting battles for God, delivering his messages and explaining things that are difficult for humans to understand.

The biblical picture is one of angels constantly, consistently, strategically engaged together with us working for our good and for the purposes of the king and the kingdom. They have personal names – we know about Michael and Gabriel – and they appear to have clear roles and responsibilities. In Exodus, the text talks about an angel that God sends before the face of his people to guard them on their way. In this passage, God declares that 'my name is in him'. We know too that there are lots of them – their scale appears vast. Jesus could call on twelve legions of angels – that's 6,000 x 12 or 72,000. We see in

Daniel similar scale: a thousand thousands serving him, and ten thousand times ten thousand who stand before him.

So it's pretty clear that these angels are present and engaged now, and although mostly invisible on earth, are pervasively involved on earth and will be highly active together with us in our stopover present heaven.

Children's angels 'always see the face of my Father who is in heaven'.[36] He is father of lights he is heavenly father so whatever the outcome, we can expect angelic engagement in the development and ageing of children in heaven. The inference is clear all through scripture, visibly and invisibly they are helping God's people. There's a cosmic war that will not be over until the end of all things – judgement, new heaven, new earth, and the final eternally permanent incarceration of Satan and his fallen angels.

Heaven is not disinterested in earth, heaven is not ignorant about earth, heaven is inextricably linked with progress on earth. Heaven and God in his heaven are surrounded by thousands of thousands of angels and heavenly beings whose role is to serve God, to worship him and to help him carry out his tasks as king and as judge.

In the hymn 'Praise My Soul the King of Heaven' we sing, 'Angels, help us to adore him; ye behold him face to face'. They are there to worship God as we will do, but that doesn't appear to be the only emphasis. From the Carpenter's lips came a prayer that should have shocked the disciples and should shock us today. We've looked at this already and this Lord's Prayer could be renamed 'A Prayer for Heaven's Hosts'. It's as if he wanted us to think about, pray about and order our lives in the context of heaven; making daily choices in the light of heaven. Your will be done on earth as what? As it is in heaven. Heaven is not a passive, worshipping sanctuary. Heaven is where God's throne is. Heaven is where the kingdom of heaven is marching forward. The throne room is not just a room for worship. Revelation shows us it's a war room; this is where stuff happens. This is where strategy is formed and articulated, this is where commands are issued, and this is where enemy plans are defeated; angels working in heaven and on earth are the troops.

With the help and engagement of angels, God in heaven calls John to heaven in Revelation in order that the things of heaven can be communicated to people on earth. To bring us reassurance. Three times, in three places he is told by an angel to write that those who die from now on in the Lord are blessed.

Twice in Revelation John falls down to worship the angel and twice the angel makes it clear, "'You must not do that! I am a fellow servant with you and your brothers who hold to the testimony of Jesus. Worship God." For the testimony of Jesus is the spirit of prophecy.'[37] 'Fellow servant' can only mean, surely, that we are both serving. What part we play may be ambiguous but one thing is clear – we play a part.

The songs of the heavenly beings (and angels) around the throne become the words of 'every creature in heaven and on earth and under the earth and in the sea'.[38] I think one of the many great benefits of a focus on heaven is that we can enter now into some of heaven's worship. Let me ask you what at first glance may feel like a somewhat strange question. If you think about your life, when are the moments you have most felt a touch of heaven? Paul speaks about tongues of men and of angels. Could it be that when we speak and sing in tongues we have a touch of heaven in that moment?

It's interesting to me that when we enter a genuine authentic time of worship in a church gathering Gill will reliably find herself in the 'throne room'. Throne room is a metaphor for prophetic experience, but it's more than a metaphor, it's a glimpse into where God is. And interestingly, on these worship-filled occasions she will often see a range of activities; commands from the throne and creatures being despatched to do the will of God. These are things that are glimpses of heaven's will for the church, the nation or for individuals. For her, as with just about every other authentic prophetic gift, the throne room is not just passive. The key is that when we engage in authentic, Christ-centred, throne-kneeling worship, we find one of those thin spaces we discussed earlier in the book, and we get a tiny glimpse of the will of God being orchestrated in heaven and being facilitated on earth.

For readers in the charismatic tradition, one of the most reliable environments to experience the presence of the Holy Spirit sent from heaven, and to enter into a thin space, is when we sing using the gift of tongues. On our own, yes, but most especially when with abandon we sing in tongues together. I think the reason for that is at least three-fold. First, you can't engage with a gift of the Holy Spirit without the Holy Spirit's presence. Second, that same Holy Spirit, as we have read, is sent from heaven. And third, Paul explains that in this context there are 'tongues of men and of angels'.[39] So when we corporately engage with a gift endowed by the Holy Spirit and sent from heaven in languages that include angelic languages and all bypassing our rational mind, little wonder that we break into heaven like Jacob on his stairway.

CHAPTER 10

Reward in Heaven

———

Every one of us loves reward. We love to know that what we have done is appreciated and has made a difference. When we engage in sport, we love to get a medal, a rosette or a certificate. It's someone else's acknowledgement of our achievement and it's meaningful.

I have never met a person in forty years as a business consultant who didn't like a bonus or a commission. Tell someone that they have earned extra because of their contribution, their hard work, their investment, their accomplishment and faces always light up. Little wonder, then, that we discover in scripture we are to be rewarded; and the knowledge of that reward is supposed to fuel our endeavours in the here and now, the every day. We saw earlier that as we pray, 'Your will be done on earth as it is in heaven', we engage with heaven's purpose here on earth. And, as with any good business, the pay and rewards structure reflect the values, the real authentic values of the company. If earth is the shadow and heaven is the reality, expect your pay and perks package to be at its best in heaven.

There is a judgement for Christians and Paul tells us, 'For we must all appear before the judgement seat of Christ, so that each of us may receive what is due to us for the things done while in the body, whether good or bad.'[1] This is not a judgement for our sins. The word used for judgement here is *bema*, which in the Greek language of the Bible was the judge's seat at the ancient games – rather like the Olympic judges' stand of today's contemporary games. And like the Olympic Games, this is where the athletes in New Testament times would receive their crowns – or in our parlance, gold, silver and bronze medals. Paul uses this very imagery elsewhere to encourage us to run the race and get the crown, and while the judgement seat belongs to the final stage of our eternal state and the day of Christ, there seems to be some overlap, and many of the passages on reward infer reward in heaven now and more fully then.

We have been told that at death we take nothing with us. That's not true, or rather it's not the whole picture! While we brought nothing material into this world and can take nothing material with us, we do in fact carry something with us when we die. While it's true that we cannot earn our entry into heaven – that's a gift we chose to either receive or reject – we definitely do determine our experience of heaven, based on the things we have done on earth. We take that investment with us into heaven, along with the relationships we have formed.

What we do on earth matters. My service matters, my attitude matters, my work matters, my relationships matter, because death is not the end of all that is good in this world, it's the beginning of eternal life that will continue, increasing and without end. When the disciples were full of the power of God and their ability to see demons despatched, probably the pinnacle of their experience to that point, Jesus makes the point in turn: 'do not rejoice in this, that the spirits are subject to you, but rejoice that your names are written in heaven.'[2] Jesus is full of focus on the will of his father in heaven and he loves to talk about reward in heaven. Reward for faithful acts, deeds and motives. Isaiah prophesied it: 'See, your Saviour comes! See, his reward is with him.'[3] Jesus said, 'For the Son of Man is going to come in his Father's glory with his angels, and then he will reward each person according to what they have done.'[4]

Paul picks up the same theme: 'God will reward each one according to the work each has done . . . But each of you must be careful how you build. For God has already placed Jesus Christ as the one and only foundation, and no other foundation can be laid. Some will use gold or silver or precious stones in building on the foundation; others will use wood or grass or straw. And the quality of each person's work will be seen when the Day of Christ exposes it. For on that Day fire will reveal everyone's work; the fire will test it and show its real quality. If what was built on the foundation survives the fire, the builder will receive a reward. But if your work is burnt up, then you will lose it; but he himself will be saved, as if he had escaped through the fire.'[5]

The fact that Paul talks quite a bit about rewards in heaven may well be due to his paradise experience. Some have speculated that his desire to depart and be with Christ is in part related to the wonder of rewards given that he had glimpsed. What we do and what we have done follows us into heaven. It's real and it has real beneficial implications.

Reward for Financial Choices

Talking to a rich young entrepreneur, Jesus challenged him to sell all he had and distribute it to the poor, and promised him treasure in heaven. The disciples were shocked that Jesus then went onto to say how hard it is for a rich person to enter the kingdom of God; almost as impossible as a camel squeezing through the eye of a needle. Peter says, 'See, we have left our homes and followed you.' But Jesus replies, 'Truly, I say to you, there is no one who has left house or wife or brothers or parents or children, for the sake of the kingdom of God, who will not receive many times more in this time, and in the age to come eternal life.'[6]

Elsewhere Jesus is even clearer: 'Lay up for yourselves treasure in heaven, where neither moth nor rust destroys and where thieves do not break in and steal. For where your treasure is, there your heart will be also.'[7] In the parable of the talents, Jesus shows us how reward in heaven is calibrated: 'Well done, good servant! Because you have been faithful in a very little, you shall have authority over ten cities.'[8] Ten minas or talents was equivalent to 10 harvest labourers for 3 months

– the reward is 10 cities. Notice that reward is not a holiday voucher – it's increased honour, with increased responsibilities and generously out of all proportion with the work or outcome that is being rewarded. Jesus' point here was about taking responsibility for what we have been given, and putting it to work for the master of heaven, serving the King of heaven with our money rather than serving earthly endeavours to get money.

In a fascinating twist, elsewhere in the gospels Jesus tells a parable about a dishonest manager, and in talking about being shrewd with money he says, 'I tell you, make friends for yourselves by means of unrighteous wealth, so that when it fails they may receive you into eternal dwellings. One who is faithful in a very little is also faithful in much . . . you cannot serve God and money.'[9] When we give to the needy, we are encouraged to do it in secret so that our father who sees in secret will reward us. Proverbs instructs us, 'Whoever is generous to the poor lends to the LORD, and he will repay him for his deed.'[10] Repayment of these loans with preferential dividends are paid in full in heaven!

It's pretty stark isn't it? We live in the wealthiest generation in history. Most of us reading this book have more disposable income, more holidays, more possessions than at any other point in history and, interestingly, we are a generation that talks little about heaven. Maybe all the money that surrounds us, fills our world, calls to us, is a distraction from seeing the will of heaven come to earth. If it is true that it is actually impossible to serve God and money, then little wonder that material wealth can so easily rob us of eternal perspective and also eternal reward. It's a paradox. Every one of us has money and we spend it, save it or invest it. How many of us transfer it into heavenly wealth or as missionary Jim Elliot once put it in a slightly different context: 'He is no fool who gives what he cannot keep to gain what he cannot lose.'[11] You can't take money with you when you die but you can certainly transfer huge deposits before you go.

Reward for Perseverance

Last words matter, really matter and I know as well as anyone just how much they matter. I find writing this moving, tearfully moving because, paraphrasing the apostle Paul, the very last words I spoke over my son's frail body were these: 'Joel David, you have fought the good fight, you have finished the race, you have kept the faith. There's a crown waiting for you. Go get it.' And as I uttered these last words, he took his very last breath and was gone from us; welcomed into heaven.

Joel had been courageous and utterly selfless in his final brutal weeks. An outstanding example of how to handle dying; persevering right to the end. Less than 24 hours earlier, he had summoned strength enough to prophecy over his friends and co-labourers in church and work. As his dad, as a follower of Jesus, as a co-labourer with him for the King of heaven, I instinctively turned to his heavenly reward as my parting gift of words, and he knew that it was his signal to weigh anchor and depart. It's bittersweet but it is true.

Paul's scripture actually calls the crown a crown of righteousness. James tells us, 'Blessed is the man who remains steadfast under trial, for when he has stood the test he will receive the crown of life, which God has promised to those who love him.'[12] Jesus said, 'Blessed are you when others revile you and persecute you and utter all kinds of evil against you falsely on my account. Rejoice and be glad, for your reward is great in heaven, for so they persecuted the prophets who were before you.'[13] 'If we endure, we will also reign with him.'[14]

This resonates with us doesn't it? When a 15-year-old is shamefully persecuted by friends and teachers alike because she believes in heterosexual marriage as the best family unit, when an airline worker is sacked for wearing a cross or an NHS worker is sacked for offering to pray for a patient, doesn't it help a bit at least to know Jesus cares, and by the way he cares enough to promise you a great reward for those moments of authentic courage?

John writing from paradise tells us, 'Be faithful unto death, and I will give you the crown of life.' 'Hold fast what you have, so that no one may seize your crown.'[15]

Crowns typically depict some state of honour or blessing for those who wear them. Quite often in both the Old and New Testament, crowns are symbols of God's blessings on his people. At times, the specific nature of that blessing is not made explicit. Blessing in scripture often carries the dual connation of favour and pleasure from God, and on a practical level, 'more of what you've got that is good.' It is ultimately God who places the crown on the king's head. As such, the king's crown may be thought of as a sign of his representative rule of what is in reality God's kingdom. These crowns are rewards and each of the rewards carry the sense of God's pleasure and favour, and at the same time open up the doorway to more responsibility and more service for the King of heaven.

Great is your reward. Great reward on earth is a shadow of what the reality looks like in heaven. More of what you have, more of what you love to do, more of what you are good at. And better yet, more without the dead weight of sin. More without the friction, the drag of selfishness, and more with the limitless empowering oil of heaven's Holy Spirit. And best of all, as on earth so in heaven, the empowering affirmation of a loving boss who tells you, 'well done', and gives you even more responsibility because you've proved yourself.

Jesus echoes this notion three times in the gospels: 'Well done, good and faithful servant. You have been faithful over a little; I will set you over much. Enter into the joy of your master.' 'Well done, good servant! You have been faithful in a very little, you shall have authority over ten cities.'[16] The montage of these scriptures shows us again that reward is more of what you've got that's good, more of what you are good at, and the ability to do it entering into the joy of your master. Work and responsibility, seeing the increase of his government forever. Work and responsibility, with his pleasure and entering into his joy – now that's work to die for!

Seeking First the Kingdom is Rewarded

'But seek first the kingdom of God and his righteousness, and all these things will be added to you.' Hebrews tells us that 'he rewards those who seek him.'[17] All those times of prayer, the daily pursuit of God in devotions, and in practical day-to-day prayers and petitions in our homes and workplaces; the seemingly unanswered cries from the heart; those occasions where, on your own or with others, you fasted, and maybe wondered afterwards if it was really all worth it.

The reward is the final answer to every question. The perspective to every painful moment or season in life, and best of all we find him – forever – and never lose him. Probably the most underrated and yet the greatest reward is proximity to Jesus himself. Everlasting joy, everlasting peace, everlasting love. Fruitful work that sees his kingdom increase, and all of that eventually in a city where we don't need the current cosmic order. No sun or moon – the light of the Lamb is all that's needed.

Mentoring, Coaching and Shepherding God's People

For the past few decades, there has been a godly emphasis on discipleship and leadership in both traditional and new or emerging churches. The latest iteration of 'huddles' follows a similar trajectory. What a joy to discover that these facets of Christian living are singled out for specific reward. Paul understood this, probably because of what he had already seen in paradise, and says this to the Thessalonians: 'What is our hope, our joy, our crown in which we will glory in the presence of our Lord Jesus when he comes? Is it not you?'[18]

Peter, talking to elders and church leaders in particular says, 'Shepherd the flock of God among you, exercising oversight, not under compulsion, but willingly, as God would have you; not for shameful gain, but eagerly; not domineering over those in your charge, but being examples to the flock. And when the chief Shepherd appears, you will receive the unfading crown of glory.'[19]

I have been an elder myself, and for four decades have worked prophetically with elders and leadership teams around the world. I know the tears that get cried, the sacrifices that are made. I see first-hand the stresses on family, finance and home life. I know so many who have been discouraged by the weight of unpopular decisions, who have fasted, prayed and paid a price for the sheep in their care. This is the normal price for those in daily leadership of our churches. There are wonderful church members who, in turn, care for and provide for pastors, leaders and their families. But in every church, these leaders will also face criticism and complaining. In other words, it's a tough job. What great news then to know that you in particular receive an unfading crown of glory.

Work Endeavours are Rewarded

Work is not a mistake and work is not a result of the fall. Work is wonderful, it's godly and, as we have seen, spills over into paradise. Eden was God's place to walk in the garden with mankind. What was that garden? It was Adam's place of work, part of God's faultless intent and design. Sin of course brought weeds to the flowerbeds and thorns to the rose, but both flowerbeds and rose were there long before sin entered with its spoiling impact. Fill the earth and subdue it was the mandate given to Adam and it is likely a similar mandate will be given for increase in paradise – and in the final destination too.

With his own trip to paradise likely bringing reminders, Paul addresses bondservants and other workers in Colossians: 'Whatever you do, work heartily, as for the Lord and not for men, knowing that from the Lord you will receive the inheritance as your reward. You are serving the Lord Christ.' He goes on to say, 'Masters treat your slaves justly and fairly, knowing that you also have a Master in heaven.'[20]

And yes, as with some of the other facets of stopover and final destination, some of these rewards seem to relate specifically to the return of Christ and the final destination. Equally, they seem to infer a pattern of reward, verbal and practical, that applies to the moment of entry into paradise. As we saw earlier, more of what you have, more of what you love to do, more of what you are good at. And better yet, more without the dead weight of sin. More without the friction, the drag of selfishness, and more with the limitless empowering oil of heaven's Holy Spirit. And best of all, as on earth, so in heaven, the empowering affirmation of a loving boss who tells you, 'Well done!' and gives you even more responsibility because you've proved yourself.

CHAPTER 11

From Stopover to Final Destination

———•———

This chapter should not be seen as a theological exposition of particular passages but rather an attempt to draw from some well-known places some facts that we can all agree on; to answer some common questions with a certainty that will bring clarity and comfort. For a full and inspired treatment of the final destination, Randy Alcorn's book *Heaven* is a must-read.

This book is focused on present heaven – paradise – but we know that this present heaven is a stopover. A wonderful, glorious, desirable, breathtakingly beautiful stopover; but stopover nonetheless, and not our final destination. We've already explored the reality that paradise is heaven's current location, it's where Jesus is right now and, importantly, it's where the throne of God is. It's the location for those who have died in faith and the destination for all those who die in faith before the return of Jesus. We know too, it is 'better by far', it is 'gain', it is the best yet. We also know, however, that it's not the final destination, and that that final destination is even better, in fact it's better by a substantial margin.

Preparations for the Final Destination

In echoes of the way Jesus described the kingdom of God or the kingdom of heaven, where one third was now, one third about the future, and one third about both, we see something similar in John's record in the book of Revelation. It seems that experience is broadly in three parts, or three phases. Firstly, in chapters 1–3, he experiences the connection between heaven and earth now. In these chapters, he is shown by the Spirit the impact of heaven on seven present-day churches and glimpses the importance of angelic activity on those churches and their development. Several times the hope of heaven is introduced, e.g. 'To the one who conquers I will grant to eat of the tree of life, which is in the paradise of God.'[1]

John is then taken though an open door up into present heaven. This second phase is marked by activity, and it's noticeable that while the remaining chapters in Revelation do include songs and words that are utterly worshipful, that is not its primary focus. John is effectively given a lengthy narrative glimpse into the activity of present heaven and provides a fascinating unfolding of how the throne, the heavenly hosts and activities on earth are all orchestrated into preparation and progress towards the final planned outcome of God's history with our planet. There appear to only be two songs sung (in all there are just 7 references to the words song, sang or singing).

What John sees primarily is activity, and that activity shows the impact of the throne, the planning and purposes of God from that throne, and a multiplicity of commands and instructions given. In response to these commands, angels are despatched, and world history is shaped and impacted.

Chapters 4 to 20 are of course a study all of their own and cover some well-known themes. Theologians have different views as to how much is past, present and future. It is also somewhat uncertain exactly how the chronology sits together. The imagery is vivid, mysterious, otherworldly and open to varying interpretations. What is certain, however, is that all these actions, activities and interventions are leading inexorably towards an end goal which is crystal clear. Here are just some of the themes:

- The magnificence of the throne and its spectacular appearance is seen to be foremost
- Heavenly creatures introduced
- The place of the Lamb and the throne brought into focus
- Seven seals introduced showing how some human beings in present heaven interact
- The prayers of the saints rise before God
- Seven trumpets announced, each one of which declares and precedes intervention from heaven into the created order – interventions that make global warming look like kindergarten
- Satan's destiny
- The harvest of the earth

- Seven angels with seven plagues
- Seven bowls of God's wrath
- The marriage supper of the Lamb
- The rider on a white horse with the armies of heaven
- The final defeat of Satan
- Judgement before the great white throne

All these themes and others are narrating a journey over time to phase three, which brings us with clarity to the final destination, and there is no better way to articulate it than to quote some extracts from the words of John himself.

The Final Destination

Then I saw a new heaven and a new earth, for the first heaven and the first earth had passed away, and the sea was no more. And I saw the holy city, new Jerusalem, coming down out of heaven from God, prepared as a bride adorned for her husband. And I heard a loud voice from the throne saying, 'Behold, the dwelling place of God is with man. He will dwell with them, and they will be his people, and God himself will be with them as their God. He will wipe away every tear from their eyes, and death shall be no more, neither shall there be mourning, nor crying, nor pain any more, for the former things have passed away.'

And he who was seated on the throne said, 'Behold, I am making all things new' . . .

And he carried me away in the Spirit to a great, high mountain, and showed me the holy city Jerusalem coming down out of heaven from God, having the glory of God, its radiance like a most rare jewel, like a jasper, clear as crystal. It had a great, high wall, with twelve gates, and at the gates twelve angels, and on the gates the names of the twelve tribes of the sons of Israel were inscribed . . .

And I saw no temple in the city, for its temple is the Lord God the Almighty and the Lamb. And the city has no need of sun or moon to shine on it, for the glory of God gives it light, and its lamp is the Lamb. By its light will the nations walk, and the kings of the earth will bring their glory into it, and its gates will never be shut by day – and there will be no night there. They will bring into it the glory and the honour of the nations. But nothing unclean will ever enter it, nor anyone who does what is detestable or false, but only those who are written in the Lamb's book of life.[2]

Then the angel showed me the river of the water of life, bright as crystal, flowing from the throne of God and of the Lamb through the middle of the street of the city; also, on either side of the river, the tree of life with its twelve kinds of fruit, yielding its fruit each month. The leaves of the tree were for the healing of the nations. No longer will there be anything accursed, but the throne of God and of the Lamb will be in it, and his servants will worship him. They will see his face, and his name will be on their foreheads. And night will be no more. They will need no light of lamp or sun, for the Lord God will be their light, and they will reign for ever and ever.[3]

Three other passages inform our thinking here and confirm the detail:

But do not overlook this one fact, beloved, that with the Lord one day is as a thousand years, and a thousand years as one day. The Lord is not slow to fulfil his promise as some count slowness, but is patient towards you, not wishing that any should perish, but that all should reach repentance. But the day of the Lord will come like a thief, and then the heavens will pass away with a roar, and the heavenly bodies will be burned up and dissolved, and the earth and the works that are done on it will be exposed.

Since all these things are thus to be dissolved, what sort of people ought you to be in lives of holiness and godliness, waiting for and hastening the coming of the day of God, because of which the heavens will be set on fire and dissolved, and the heavenly bodies will melt as they burn! But according to his promise we are waiting for new heavens and a new earth in which righteousness dwells. [4]

Behold! I tell you a mystery. We shall not all sleep, but we shall all be changed, in a moment, in the twinkling of an eye, at the last trumpet. For the trumpet will sound, and the dead will be raised imperishable, and we shall be changed.[5]

But we do not want you to be uninformed, brothers, about those who are asleep, that you may not grieve as others do who have no hope. For since we believe that Jesus died and rose again, even so, through Jesus, God will bring with him those who have fallen asleep. For this we declare to you by a word from the Lord, that we who are alive, who are left until the coming of the Lord, will not precede those who have fallen asleep. For the Lord himself will descend from heaven with a cry of command, with the voice of an archangel, and with the sound of the trumpet of God. And the dead in Christ will rise first. Then we who are alive, who are left, will be caught up together with them in the clouds to meet the Lord in the air, and so we will always be with the Lord. Therefore encourage one another with these words.[6]

The first pages of scripture talk about a God who would walk with his creation on earth. God's desire, his design, his intent has always been to live with us. The fall destroyed that design and God and man were separated on earth and in heaven. These very last pages show God bringing heaven down to earth, a totally renewed earth. God's desire, his design, his intent has always been to live with us. And in these final descriptions of the ultimate destination, we see just that.

The Journey from Paradise

Those of us who die before the return of Christ go to paradise or present heaven. We have described this as the stopover, and we are in a temporary body or form, a stopover body. When the trumpet sounds, the voice of the archangel sounds and the end comes. Those of us that have died get preferential treatment; our bodies get raised first, spirit and resurrection body are united, and together with those still living on earth we meet Christ together in the air. From that point, and now in our resurrection bodies, new bodies, we move to our new address, our final destination: new heaven, new earth, new Jerusalem.

The writer to the Hebrews, talking of earth and the heavens, says: 'They will perish, but you remain; they will all wear out like a garment, like a robe you will roll them up, like a garment they will be changed.'[7] We inhabit this new heaven and new earth in amazing new resurrection bodies that bear the image of Jesus and will be like Jesus, with all the amazing supernatural qualities that Jesus' body had. Jesus didn't float, he walked, and his feet touched the ground. He could barbeque fish, maybe even bait a hook or cast a net to catch those fish. He ate and drank with his friends and his supernaturally changed body still appeared recognizable with hands and feet, and nail wounds and a wound in his side. This body could appear and disappear. This same body could travel effortlessly from one place to another and move through walls. This is a body that somehow carries continuity with the old, with our stories, but is totally, powerfully, miraculously transformed.

Bodies that were sown perishable are raised imperishable, bodies sown in dishonour are raised in glory, sown in weakness and raised in power.[8] What a hope! What a body! What a home! What a great location!

CHAPTER 12

Death Without a Sting

———

Gill came back from a craft evening recently and told me that one of her friends, Debbie, had said to her, 'So glad you weren't there last Sunday.' When pressed, Debbie expanded, 'Nearly all the songs were about heaven and the grave and death.' Debbie understood something, and in her love for Gill reflected her understanding. Since Joel has died, every Sunday gathering we have attended, there have been songs about death and heaven. Every Sunday.

And it's painful. Not because I disagree with the theology, but because the singing and the words themselves touch memories, touch the wellspring of grief still ready and waiting to pour out its tears. And mostly I can't sing. Not because I lack faith in the concept but because the painful reality of Joel's dying comes flooding back into my mind like a 3D IMAX and I'm back there with him. Debbie instinctively understood that and wanted to protect her friend from that.

But here I am at a keyboard, just five short months after joining arms with Joel's son and Joel's brother and together carrying my son Joel's coffin into the crematorium. And yes, I really do want to talk about death without a sting. Not death without grief but death as God sees it, death as Joel now sees it.

As you are reading this, I suspect your mind is already wrestling with a scripture. It's almost certainly in your mind right now, and you are possibly even feeling empathy with me and our family, but wondering about this scripture. The scripture of course is: "'Death is swallowed up in victory.' 'O death, where is your victory? O death, where is your sting?' The sting of death is sin . . . But thanks be to God, who gives us the victory through our Lord Jesus Christ.'[1]

This is Paul writing. Paul, who had already been to paradise and had a glimpse so profoundly attractive of present heaven, that he was given a thorn in the flesh to keep him earthbound for a while. Paul, who as we saw earlier knew and proclaimed that to die is gain. This is Paul who was itching to depart and be with Christ which is 'far better'. That's not just nice words in an ancient text – that is heart-stopping, jaw-dropping revelation. I would like to draw two things out from this text, which at the time had the philosophical impact of a nuclear bomb. This was explosive new truth on the biggest scale. Jesus himself had opened the door to this new thinking when he said, 'Blessed are those who mourn, for they shall be comforted.'[2] But Paul is developing it into something even more impacting.

In the ancient world, if you could be certain of one thing in your three score years and ten it would be that death would have the final say and death would swallow up all you were and all you had done. Death was considered the great 'swallower'.

It swallowed all human life, it was a penal event that followed sin in the created world. But now Paul is saying that with the resurrection of Christ death itself is swallowed up. The victory of Christ has put to an end forever the power of death. Death itself is defeated.

The context for this game-changing Pauline pronouncement is also found in an earlier verse where, with his mind, his memory and his emotions, Paul is probably reaching back to his near death experience and says this: 'flesh and blood cannot inherit the kingdom of God, nor does the perishable inherit the imperishable.'[3]

So actually, death hurts and it hurts bad – but only for those left behind. In the short term, death stings those left behind and stings bad. And in that context, don't expect the grieving friends or relatives to sing along with you as you sing with confidence, 'Oh death where is your sting?' That's not what Paul is talking about here. He is talking about what happens to the dying person after he or she has breathed their last breath. That's his focus in this text. To an unbeliever, the thought of death is terrifying, or should be. But for those who have peace with God, death is the doorway into 'far better'; death is the gateway to home.

In his book *One Minute After You Die*, Erwin Lutzer says Death for the dying person is a gift, not an enemy. If Adam and Eve had eaten of the tree of life, they would have been immortalized in their sinful condition. They never would have qualified for heaven, which God wanted them to enjoy. Eden paradise would have been lost to them forever. God gave the gift of death, the ability to exit this life and arrive safely at the 'far better' life to come.

Death though it appears to be man's greatest enemy, would in the end prove to be his greatest friend. I know it's a shocking thought but it's the ultimate liberation. I cannot go to heaven the way I am, only through death can we go to God. Think of how utterly powerless death is; rather than robbing us of wealth it introduces us to eternal wealth. Rather than poor health pain abuse or old age, death gives us immediate access to the tree of life in paradise for eternal healing not just for me but also for the nations. No matter how alert and primed, no matter how wealthy or poor, no matter how we have showered and dressed we are not fit for heaven. You can't have a decaying body in a permanent home.

Only on this side of the curtain is death our enemy. Just beyond the curtain, the monster turns out to be our friend. The label 'Death' is still on the bottle, but the contents are 'Life Eternal'. Death is our friend because it reminds us that heaven is near. How near? As near as a heartbeat; as near as an auto accident; as near as a stray bullet; as near as a plane crash. If our eyes could see what Gehazi, Stephen, and Jacob saw we might find we are already at heaven's gates

Death then is not the *end* of the road; it is only a *bend* in the road. The road winds only through those paths through which Christ Himself has gone . . .

The tomb is not an entrance to death, but to life. The sepulchre is not an empty vault, but the doorway to heaven.[4]

God's Loving Kindness is Better than Life

I remember when my dad died. I was 21 and had the privilege of nursing him with Mum. We had fought over six long months for his recovery, we had prayed and fasted for his healing, and then the end came close. I remember going through stages of anger, sadness, fighting the seeming injustice of it all. The night he died, I was sleeping downstairs, not far away from his bed. He actually died while we were both asleep. When I woke up, I heard no breathing, and looked across at my first sight of death.

In the shock of it all, in my nervous unpreparedness, something happened. I found myself kneeling at the foot of the bed on which he lay, sensing the presence of God and his angels. I found myself singing, 'Thy loving kindness is better than life, thy loving kindness is better than life, my lips shall praise thee, thus will I bless thee, thy loving kindness is better than life. I lift my hands up unto thy name, I lift my hands up unto thy name, my lips will praise thee, thus will I bless thee, I lift up my hands unto thy name.'[5] Somehow God breathed his perspective into my heart and mind, right at the time when I needed it most.

Widowed, orphaned, bereaved father or mother, or a sibling still feeling the pain over a brother or sister lost – his loving kindness is better than life. He said it; we can trust it. Perhaps hardest of all, those of you who have the pain of a stillborn baby, a cot death, a young child taken from you. His loving kindness is better than life.

My first experience of death was to be life changing in a number of ways and, of course, in part prepared me for what was to come with Joel. Four scriptures became part of my foundation, they shaped my thinking and informed the subsequent forty years of pastoral input into others who would walk this path. I have already shared the first.

1. 'Your loving kindness is better than life'[6]

When a loved one is dying, everything in us wants them to be healed, to live, to get better. It's because their life right there, right then is the most important thing in our minds, and of course, it's understandable. But as we explore this, we begin to see and maybe believe that God's purpose for our loved ones and for us is faultless and not a mistake. His lovingkindness, however we feel right now, maybe for many years to come, is going to work all things together for good, it really is. His loving kindness will always be greater than our unanswered questions.

2. 'Blessed are those who mourn, for they shall be comforted'[7]

Hundreds upon hundreds of times I have seen these words straight from the lips of Jesus make a difference. Like other scriptures, it's important we don't have a single approach to this. For those left behind, the scripture tells us, it is dark. The psalmist calls it 'the valley of the shadow of death'.[8] In Hebrew, the proper rendition of that sentence is 'the valley of deepest darkness'. But in that darkest of all valleys, we also are promised comfort. Comfort in our tears. Comfort in hope-infused grief that helps heal, rather than adding to the darkness. At countless funerals, thanksgiving services and committals, I have witnessed the presence of the Holy Spirit strengthening and protecting even the most vulnerable of widows, orphans and bereaved parents, and in the most utterly tragic of circumstances. And somehow, into all of that normal and natural emotion comes the anaesthetic of the comfort of God. In the process, somehow grieving takes on a positive dimension. It is not just the normal and proper way in which our bodies adjust to change and cope with the loss. It is a heaven-breathed process uniquely ours for this season in which God's presence is somehow at its richest, its closest, its most real. There is nothing more valuable on earth than the powerful comforting presence of the Holy Spirit. If Jesus said it himself, most of us can find enough faith to believe it and ask for that comfort.

The day our family was dreading the most was Joel's committal and thanksgiving service. During the long wait of more than two weeks over Christmas, the day was looming large for all of us. And yet I watched with grateful awe as each family member – Joel's widow Joanna, Joel's children Jacob and Daisy, Joel's siblings Carleen, Joshua and Cheryl-Ann, and Gill and me – was given a strength, a courage and a peace that was and is inexplicable. Jacob, at the age of 13, gave a thoughtful, inspired and moving tribute. Joshua and I were able to read our tributes with strength, courage and anointing to the packed church of many hundreds. Over 1,200 people have subsequently listened to the tribute online.[9] Yes, there were tears and moments of deepest sadness, but God was honoured, God was present, and the promise from the lips of the carpenter two millennia earlier was evident. 'Blessed are those who mourn, for they shall be comforted.'

3. 'Precious in the sight of the LORD is the death of his faithful servants. Truly I am your servant, LORD; I serve you just as my mother did; you have freed me from my chains.'[10] I don't know what chains the psalmist was thinking of, but I suspect it included a wrong view of death. God says death is precious for those that belong to him. God is speaking to us and saying, 'Don't view it negatively, because I don't. View it as precious, view it as glorious, view it as highly valued.' Precious is a word I would normally use relationally with Gill or with one of our children, usually at times of great closeness or affection. This is at the heart of this statement: it's God's affectionate heart saying, 'You're coming home and I love you.' This is a precious moment.

Satan designed death as the greatest horror, the icy hand, the fear-filled journey to doom, the dark valley of foreboding. But God says, 'It is precious in my sight.' These are victory words.

4. 'I am the Living One; I was dead, and now look, I am alive for ever and ever! And I hold the keys of death and Hades.'[11] He decides when the time is right. He decides when the lock turns. Satan's shadowy hand may be involved, but the Master, the Lord over death, controls the time, the process and the destination for every individual. Every family and every person will handle the moment differently. Some are ready to go, are at peace about it and know the time is right. They are just ready to give up the ghost, to yield their spirits into the hands of God. Others, like Joel and us his family, will fight to the very end, look for healing, believe for healing. And if they should die in the process, is that failure? Is that some kind of lack of faith? Is that because of sin? Is it some great disaster from which the church should reel in shock? No!

The moment Joel slipped into the next world Satan wanted to shout, 'I've done it, I've got him.' Jesus proclaims, 'He is mine, all mine, safely mine, mine for ever.' Our grief, deep and painful as it is and will be, is temporary. From the very first minute it was tinged with the colour of victory. As a family, with God's help we will finish our own race to be run, we will climb our own mountains. But in eternal terms, it is such a short time, and then we will be with him again. Then there will be a whole new eternity of destiny and function to get stuck into together.

The healing ministry does not hold the keys of death and hell. The church does not hold the keys of death and hell. Who does? An Almighty omniscient God, who knows everything right down to the deep stirrings of the orphaned child, the loneliness of the grieving spouse, the grown-up children who feel bereaved that their father or mother has gone in some way early.

Who holds the keys? An omnipotent God. All-powerful. He does release healing but not to everyone and not in every situation. Even when healing is released, no matter how miraculously, every healed person who has ever walked this earth has subsequently died. Every person raised from the dead – and there have been plenty – still has to face the frontier of death. In the gospels, Jesus raised three people from the dead – they still had to die! He knows the time.

Who holds the keys? A magnificent saviour who can't wait to welcome us home. A loving God who says there is a future beyond death that is far more wonderful and fantastic than you can even imagine – painful as the separation might be.

A Theology to be Faced

There is an issue to be settled, a nettle to be grasped, a theology to be faced and a view of death to be filled with faith. Our faith is not just in the place – a wonderful paradise – but also in the timing of our arrival. 'It is appointed for man to die once, and after that comes judgement'.[12] He really does hold the keys of death and hell. No one will pluck them from his hands.

So it is that we are challenged to face the question, do we believe, truly believe that God chooses the time of our loved one's death? And if we do believe that, then we don't depart for heaven because of cancer or a road accident, but we die in faith that this is our time to go. Yes, of course we take appropriate safety precautions, and yes, we pray for healing and take all the medical intervention we can get. But in the end, and at the end, he is sovereign, he does hold the keys and he will have the final word.

I met with Andy the pastor of our church recently to share with him our journey with Joel. Several times during the brutal sickness and constant trips to the North to be with our family, Andy had tried to reach out and offer support and prayer. I wanted to share with him something of the pain and challenge of our journey and explain to him why we hadn't responded much to his kind and authentic offers of help. We had good dialogue and Andy came prepared with questions of his own, and at some length we talked through the process of shock and trauma, and the implications of both on our grief as individuals and as a family.

Today, just two weeks later, I have returned to my office from a long walk with Andy. His father had a sudden heart attack just four days after our conversation. Andy shared with me some of the details. His dad (nicknamed Thompy) arrived around 9 a.m. to help run a discipleship day in his local church. He was busy setting out refreshments for the delegates when he collapsed. Uniquely, for this event only, because of the subject matter there were four doctors and three nurses attending this course, who began CPR quite literally within seconds of his collapse. They were able to run the CPR on a skilled rotation, giving the best possible chance of recovery. Within fifteen minutes or so, an ambulance arrived with defibrillator and continued in attendance before blue-lighting him to hospital.

Over a number of days, the hospital placed Thompy in an induced coma and then allowed him to come out of that, keeping him sedated enough to keep an airway in. By the Thursday of the following week, it was clear that there was likely to be some brain damage, and by Saturday the family had been called in to be told the worst. At this briefing, Andy noticed a nurse who was 'new'. The nurse was introduced as an organ donor nurse and the conversation began with the family about potential organ donation.

Thompy had carried an organ donor card and the family was quickly unanimous in agreeing to the donation. Arrangements were made, and it was agreed that once donor logistics were in place, the artificial respirator would be turned off. Donor matches were found within hours and the potential recipients were made ready.

A specialist transplant surgeon (one of only a handful in the UK) was drafted in from Oxford. To the amazement of Andy's family, it was discovered that the surgeon, James Gilbert, was a family friend and knew Thompy and his wife Gill well. He came into the ward and embraced Gill before going to theatre to ready himself and the team. The family had been told that in order for major organs – liver and kidneys – to be used, death needed to occur within three hours of the artificial respirator being turned off. The machine was turned off on Sunday morning and the family prayed for God to take Thompy home within the three-hour period. They had worship music playing and continuous prayer. You can understand, then, that it was a huge disappointment when the three-hour mark had passed, rendering the organs unusable.

The sadness for the family was acute, and as Thompy continued to breathe unaided they left the hospital room at 11 p.m. to get much needed rest, assuming that he would continue until the next morning. In fact, at 3 a.m. the family got a call from the hospital to say that Thompy had passed away.

Andy's shock, sadness and grief were compounded by questions. Why did God allow him to die after the organs were no longer viable? Having apparently lined up the Christian friend who was the surgeon, why did God allow Thompy to carry on 'living' when it would have made such a difference to donor recipients and to the family? And why then take him at 3 a.m. when the family were all at home.

We cried together and prayed together, and I shared with Andy the essence of this chapter.

Ultimately, only one person in the universe determines the exact second of our last breath. If Jesus authentically holds the keys of death and the afterlife, then only he can turn them. If it is appointed for a man to die once, then that appointment, that moment of departure is significant in ways that we may never fully understand on earth. If it is true that the King of heaven will have the last say, will have the last word, then that includes the timing of angels released to escort the loved one to heaven.

I said to Andy, 'I am in awe over the timing and kindness of God in this. You and I met and had the conversation we had just four days before Thompy's collapse. Thompy had walked to the church and was actually in the church when he collapsed, not on a road or pavement somewhere else. There were four medics and three nurses attending the event who did immediate CPR. The ambulance with defibrillator was there within 15 minutes. The eminent donor transplant surgeon was a family friend and was the one invited to operate.'

As I reflected on these things, they appeared to me as the unmistakable fingerprints of heaven. Unmistakeably, the King of heaven was making it clear that Thompy had the best possible, the best imaginable care. When Jesus chose the precise moment, Andy and his family could be certain and confident that if Jesus could orchestrate all those things, there was no accident, this was the timing of God. We may never know on earth the precise reasons why God chose for those donors not to receive those organs, but he did. We may never know why God took Thompy home while the family wasn't there, but he did.

Erwin Lutzer in his book says:

Listen to the conversation at almost any funeral and you will hear some 'if onlys'.

'*If only* we had called the doctor sooner . . .'
'*If only* there had not been ice on the highway . . .'
'*If only* we had noticed the lump sooner . . .'
'*If only* they had operated . . .'
'*If only* they had not operated . . .'

Let me encourage you to take those 'if onlys' and draw a circle around them. Then label the circle 'The Providence of God'. The Christian believes that God is greater than our 'if onlys'. His providential hand encompasses the whole of our lives, not just the good days but the 'bad' days too. We have the word *accident* in our vocabulary; he does not.

Accidents, ill health, or even dying at the hand of the enemy – God uses all these means to bring his children home. As long as we entrust ourselves to his care, we can be confident that we are dying according to his timetable . . . The fact is God can send any chariot he wishes to fetch us for himself.[13]

I shared these thoughts with Andy and remarked that for Thompy death was a gift, sending him on his way to eternal life in the presence of the Master he had faithfully served. And that in God's eyes that moment of death was and is precious. We of course are left in the valley of deepest darkness. We are left to puzzle, anguish and grieve. Thompy rejoices and, even if he could, he would never return.

I understand these 'if onlys'. With Joel's death there were many along the way, and even more at the very end. They are a natural response. But somewhere, at some point, whatever my pain and however intense my grief, my convictions will surface – Jesus really does hold the keys to death, and he is sovereign, and he really does have the last word.

Having read the NDEs and been at the death of my father, my son, my mother-in-law and countless church members, I have some unanswered questions. Why is it that God gives some a near death experience and then sends them back? Why does he take others without even the slightest hint of the presence of angels? Only God can ever clarify that fully. But if we believe that he holds the keys, if we believe he has the last word then, as Spurgeon put it: 'When we cannot trace God's hand, we must trust God's heart.'

Mother Theresa once said, 'In light of heaven, the worst suffering on earth, a life full of the most atrocious tortures on earth, will be seen to be no more serious than one night in an inconvenient hotel.'[14]

Our future existence is not in the hands of treatments, surgeons, miracle cures or their lack. My life is not in the hands of the gunman or the drunk driver. My life has always been and will always be in the hands of the Almighty. He will have the last word, he holds the keys and he can and does determine when I take my last breath here and my next breath somewhere else. Ecclesiastes tell us, 'No man has power to retain the spirit, or power over the day of death.'[15]

I know for many, if not all, the inevitable question is, 'Why?' Maybe a better question is 'What for?' I found peace by asking God these questions: 'What is it that I can do now because of Joel's death that I couldn't do before?' and 'What is it that I should do now because of Joel's death that I couldn't do before?' This book is one tiny response to the answers to those questions.

Dying is Different

While the theology of death for the departing one can bring some perspective, even some solace, I don't want to trivialize the horror of dying. While death will be a gift to the one travelling to heaven, dying is very different. No one I have ever met looks forward to the process of dying. And we should not feel guilty for facing the dying process with some apprehension.

Even Jesus experienced distress as he contemplated his dying, crying out to his father, sweating, as it were, great drops of blood.

The procedures that Joel endured; the pain that our family had to witness while caring for him; the shocking lack of pain relief in some settings; the fight to get the appropriate treatment; the rapid deterioration of his body; and the multiple painful interventions. Several times Joel who was the bravest, most courageous person I have ever met said, 'I feel like I have been tortured for weeks' and 'I feel like I have been savaged by dogs'. Those are harrowing experiences for the dying person and equally for the family members caring for them.

There is a sting in death and that sting is in the immediate for those who are left. The dying process can often add to that stinging, painful experience. That's where 'good grief' can be a help, and that's our final chapter.

CHAPTER 13

Good Grief

———•———

Our grieving began long before Joel died. The family's soul received a thousand cuts as we journeyed with him. Tense waits for blood and tissue results. The imperfect NHS groaning and creaking at its seams. Delayed treatment, delayed pain relief, delayed diagnoses, delayed prognosis.

Brutal treatments took their toll on us daily, especially in the last 17 days of Joel's fight. We had to witness his cries of pain, witness with immense pride the fortitude with which he conducted himself. We had to learn to hold back our own tears, as he selflessly prepared his business staff, his church co-labourers and his own family.

Multiple shocks would take our breath away. I remember the short-lived joy one evening of getting a call from Joel. He was sitting with his wife Joanna, and Gill. They had just had an evening call from the consultant. 'Good news, we have the test results – it's not lymphoma, it's not cancer.' Over the next three weeks the pain and symptoms increased. Further tests followed, and we learnt after pushing, negotiating, pleading for investigations that it might be operable bowel cancer, and our hopes were raised.

Then came the day. My daughter Cheryl-Ann had called in the morning to say it was looking likely that my mother was going to die imminently. She and her sister Carleen were going to try and get there in time to be with her. I rushed home from a business meeting but didn't make it in time. As I sat in our lounge at home, there was a knock at the door. Both of my daughters stood at the door with a few of my mother's possessions at the very moment that Joel called and told us through his own tears that he had cancer. A few days later he called again to tell us that he had only two weeks to six months to live. Seventeen exhausting days later, he was safe in the arms of Jesus, and we were bereft.

Grief in those circumstances can come like an express train, or it can seep out through tears like barely imperceptible drops of sap from a tree's bark. It can cause you to shout, to cry out, to bury your head into a friend's arms. It can descend like a mist of perpetual darkness and it can catch you out when you least expect it. It can leave you in shock and disbelief. It can fill your mind with anger. It follows you to bed and fills your sleep and dreams. It plays back pictures to process the trauma and tries to help your mind make sense of it all. All these things and much more belong to grief.

Occasionally you may get caught up in a virtual tsunami of grief where, for some reason, from deep within erupts a tidal wave of emotion that you weren't expecting, don't fully understand, and certainly can't resist. There are moments which professionals call 'readiness,' when a number of contributing factors are in place and an unexpected tsunami of grief might positively take place.

Gill and I had the privilege of staying with Alasdair and Eleanor Fulton. Eleanor is a retired clinical psychologist. They housed us while Joel was in his last days and helped us facilitate the 24-hour family care. When Gill and I rang the doorbell at their home in Hilton, in the North of England, we both crumbled, and for several hours our unstoppable tears provided the river along which we could push the boat of our questions, pain and uncertainties. Gill would say afterwards that it was if we handed Eleanor all the broken pieces of the vase of our life and within those first few hours, she had glued them back together sufficiently to enable us to carry on.

Psalm 23 tells us that 'though I walk through the valley of the shadow of death, I will fear no evil, for you are with me; your rod and your staff, they comfort me.' The Hebrew rendering of that phrase is 'the valley of deepest darkness'. Eleanor explained to us that grief is like a long black tunnel, pitch-black and with no apparent light visible at the end. Occasionally, she suggested, just occasionally, you may see tiny pinpricks of light that last for a moment, a second or two.

Jesus Understands the Pain of Loss and Grief

The death of one of Jesus' closest friends, Lazarus, actually produced the shortest verse in the Bible. 'When Jesus saw her weeping, and the Jews who had come along with her also weeping, he was deeply moved in his spirit and greatly troubled. "Where have you laid him?" They said to him, "Lord, come and see." *Jesus wept.* So the Jews said, "See how he loved him!"'[1]

Jesus had lost his own father sometime after the age of 12, exactly when we are not sure. With all the positive statements we have made, Jesus does not minimize the pain of grief. He does not whitewash over it, he can share in it intimately. And in this short story with the shortest verse in the Bible, we get it. Jesus understands grief. He, more than anyone, knows that death is conquered, but it still leaves widows, orphans and bereaved parents behind. At the cross there is a remarkable exchange where he makes preparation, and says to Mary, 'Behold, your son!' and to John, 'Behold, your mother!' Whatever else was being set up, Jesus understood the importance of close, trustworthy support at a time of grief.

If you were to ask anyone who grieves the death of a loved one, one of the things they feel is that they grieve alone, that no one really understands them. That is often true on a human level, but the liberating truth is that in our deepest pain, in those ceaseless seeping tears or in a tsunami of grief, Jesus has been there and understands it.

We read about Stephen's martyrdom, and when he finally died, after a brutal and painful death, we read, 'Devout men buried Stephen and made great lamentation over him.'[2]

In Philippians, the Apostle Paul notes that, 'God had mercy on him, and not on him only but also on me, to spare me sorrow upon sorrow.'[3] Paul was already sorrowful over those who had died, and he was grateful at that moment not get a double dose!

Grief and love are woven together. Our grief is only so intense because of how intense the love was. One of Jacob's friends said to him, you would have been better off if you'd had a dad who beat you and never loved you, but your dad was so wonderful, so loving and so creative with memories, you will miss him like mad.

Joel and I were so close, whenever we spent time together working commercially in church settings or just having adventures, it was light and life and love for both of us. When one or the other had to travel five hours to return home, there would be the dull ache of temporary loss and a keen awareness of the sadness of parting. When Gill and I moved to America, it was a painful parting for each of our four children in different ways. If we feel that temporary parting so keenly, how much more shall we, and should we, miss those that Jesus takes from us.

Isaiah, in a well-known often-read passage, talks about an anointing for healing (binding up) the broken-hearted.[4] And Psalms talks about saving the crushed in spirit.[5] In this context, it is evident that sorrow and grief are to be expected and, actually, welcomed. Really? Yes, if he is to heal the broken-hearted, then expect tears. If he is to heal the crushed in Spirit, then expect tears. Tears can be either a symptom or a sign of grief without hope, or they can reflect real, deep even unimaginable loss, and yet with hope and a certainty about both the destination of our loved one and the certainty of our own healing.

Not All Christians Get It

Some Christians have mistakenly thought that grief demonstrates a lack of faith. That way they feel the need to maintain strength rather than deal honestly with painful loss. Others simply cannot understand the depth of pain that widows, orphans and bereaved parents exhibit. It's as if they want things to get back to normal! That normal doesn't exist any more for the bereaved family or person, and it never will.

Others will even quote the verse and lustily sing it alongside a grieving widow in church: 'Oh grave, where is your victory, oh death, where is your sting?' We have seen this in the previous chapter: death stings and stings bad and proper. Understanding of that scripture might make a big difference in how we treat those in our churches who are grieving.

I said to Gill at one point, 'Wouldn't it just help to cry more and get it over?' She replied, 'It's like a bucket trying to empty an ocean. That's how much difference it would actually make. Good grief is necessary, biblical, godly, and to be encouraged. In Chapter 11, we looked at the words of Jesus himself: 'Blessed are those who mourn, for they shall be comforted.' That is both a promise from the lips of the all-powerful creator and it is also an invitation to the people of God to be part of that comfort. Either way, for there to be the promised comfort there has to be mourning. Mourning is tears, loud cries, shouts, unimaginable pain and a continuing dark, shadowy, overcast sense of loss.

'Good grief doesn't go away. You can supress it, ignore it, busy it away, hide from it, run from it, but it will lay there hidden away until one day it will find its own way out.'[6]

Good grief is the grief that enables us to make the transition to a new phase of existence. Yes, the widow must learn to live alone and the parents must bear the unimaginable sense of loneliness brought on by the death of their son or daughter. Siblings must struggle as the often-forgotten mourners, as they lose the love of their brother or sister; and children perhaps toughest of all, must handle the loss of one or both parents. Grief that deals honestly with the pain is part of the healing process.

So life will never be 'normal' again. It is said often, and it's very true – you don't move on, you move forward with your grief. Some bereaved folk say it is like losing a limb – you will never be fully healed but you learn to live differently and learn to adapt.

Grief disables you. You can still do things, but your abilities are not what they were. I think that Gill's and my mental acuity is running at around 70 per cent of normal. Our physical and emotional strength and well-being probably less than 70 per cent. That's the reality of grief. I still have a rainbow of emotions. I still do have red, blue, indigo, but now there's a band of black that was not there before – part of my life is black now.

Stephen Curtis Chapman, talking about his album *The Glorious Unfolding*, described the pain that doubles up as we wake up each day to the fresh awareness of loss. Wondering if he would scream enough that his voice would go. Like Gill and me, he forced himself to say, 'Blessed be the name of the Lord'.

This sculpture by Albert György, entitled 'Melancholy', can be found beside Lake Geneva in Switzerland. It sums up bereavement.

John Maddox, a Kansas pastor, speaking about how he feels after his daughter's death says, 'We may look as if we carry on with our lives as before. We may even have times of joy and happiness. Everything may seem "normal". But this "emptiness" is how we all feel . . . all the time.'

People have asked, and a number have implied the question, 'Are you over it yet?' It's quite shocking when you are on the receiving end. I had one newly bereaved daughter-in-law in our church after one week, yes one week, say that church members were implying to her that she would be 'over it soon'. Christians often feel or others incline them to feel guilty over long-continuing tears of bereavement. Sometimes other well-meaning church members try to almost force an unreal spirituality because they feel we should 'live up to it'. Why? Because apparently the comfort of the Spirit should be sufficient to dry tears. However, the fact is that the drying of tears does not happen until heaven, *QED*. In fact, the more like Jesus we are, the more we will be like Jesus at the tomb of Lazarus. We are allowed to weep, it is expected, and he even gathers our tears into his bottle.[7]

I'm not judging here either. Countless times I have had that lump of concrete in the pit of my stomach as I approach a bereaved person or family, crying to God, 'Please give me some words'. It's hard, and we often don't know what to say. One of the most helpful moments for Gill and me was when our friend Rob Parsons came to visit us. He listened for over an hour and a half, gave no advice, told us one short story. But he wept with us and said the most meaningful thing anyone could say: 'I have no clever words and even my prayer on the way here wasn't clever. All I could pray was, "Lord let me do them no harm."'

Words can occasionally help, often they are neutral, sometimes they even do damage (like 'Are you over it yet?') But what we can all do is by our presence weep with those who weep. Our presence and our tears can say more than words will ever communicate.

For Those Left Behind, a Few Words

The Bible is full of promises and helpful perspectives, but you may well find a struggle to even read or benefit from scripture like you once did

'Grief is not sharp and pointed, it's grey and flat, like a fog, and because you can't see it, you don't know why life seems so dreary.'[8] In her novel *Shadow on the Land*, Anne Doughty expresses this with careful feeling:

> At the thought of heaven, she shivered. There would be a funeral, a service, a eulogy from the local minister. Yards and yards of pious reassurance that the parting was temporary and it was all part of God's plan . . . No wonder Alex didn't believe any of it. She wasn't sure she'd got much belief left either though she noticed that she'd never stopped praying . . . often enough over the kitchen sink or the ironing board she caught herself asking for strength.[9]

It's okay to struggle, and in fact it's quite normal. And it's good to know you have permission to take all the time you need. People vary so greatly in terms of how they grieve. We met with one friend for whom it was more than twelve months before she could even contemplate returning to a church gathering. Gill and I had to think it through really carefully.

The hardest part of church re-entry is the challenge of meeting scores of well-meaning people, and the process of conversation can be negative and utterly draining. What we did was to arrive two or three minutes late, asking someone to keep seats right by the door, and we would leave at the start of the last song or at the start of the closing prayer. After several months, we were able to stay and talk for five minutes, though even that was demanding. We put a notice in our church newsletter explaining and also advising people how they could 'handle us'. Even with that careful preparation, most services have still posed a challenge and have not in the main been helpful. But neither Gill nor I wanted to retreat totally.

It's also important to understand how differently we need to express and deal with our grief. In the early weeks, Gill needed to speak to people, sometimes at length. Whereas speaking to numbers of different people was very challenging and unhelpful for me. Church members and church leaders quite rightly wanted to visit. Gill was grateful; I was challenged. In the end, we explained to visitors that I found talking to multiple people draining and unhelpful, whereas Gill found it to be a blessing. She would then spend time with all the visitors and I would come in at the end of any time and gladly benefit from the prayer. Friends understood, and both of us in the end found that helpful.

I had and still have one or two key friends who know the whole story, and who form my closest network of support, and they pray with me and for me. That's enough. It's the right balance for me of sharing my journey but not too often and not with too many.

Professional counselling, especially from Christian sources can be immensely helpful. Some in our family have benefitted especially from this help. What is critical is having prayer support and being unashamed to request it and receive it. During Joel's illness and the subsequent months, we felt like the most prayed-for family on the planet and we were so grateful for that support and the friends who administrated emails and updates to ensure that this support was in place and was happening.

We like Tennyson, we long 'for the touch of a vanished hand, and the sound of a voice that is still.'[10]

But heaven has given our broken hearts a heart-warming hope: 'Then eyes with joy will sparkle, that brimmed with tears of late; orphans no longer fatherless, nor widows desolate.' There will be 'knitting severed friendships up where partings are no more.'[11] But the reality is that however we plan and adapt, good grief will carry you along.

Joel and all those Christians who have gone before have been reunited with friends and family. They have already met Bible characters they and we have loved. They have begun to relate to the millions and millions who have gone before from every tribe and tongue and nation. For them all it truly is 'Better by far' and for those of us left behind it's good and right to be 'Always going home inside'.

I have already shared the very last words I spoke to Joel on earth, before he took his last breath here and his next in the arms of Jesus in paradise. Let me close out this chapter with my declaration spoken over Joel just before my very last words.

The Lord gives and the Lord takes away. Blessed be the name of the Lord.

Good night son, see you in the morning X

If you would like to listen to the family tributes broadcast for Joel Oliver, visit:

http://bit.ly/DavidTribute
http://bit.ly/Familytribute

Acknowledgements

Thank you to Joanna's family, June, Duncan and Emma. Hundreds of leaders and church members from our church family have stood with us in prayer, reaching out to us multiple ways and to you, the body of Christ, we say a heartfelt thank you. Steve Thomas, you read the first draft of this book and helped enormously with content and theology.

To Dave and Rachel Rebbettes, Andy and Sharon Forbes, Martin and Linda Dunkley, Alasdair and Eleanor Fulton, Doctor Ola Afolabi, Simon and Glenys Hart, Antony & Dorothy Kelton, Dan Richards and the Bishop Auckland Elim team, Dave and Mandy Mallon, Ros Smith.

You stood with us, often daily, in the darkest moments of our lives and shone the light of heaven on our path. You supported us and strengthened us to face the toughest, most brutal of storms.

We would not have made it without you.

APPENDIX I

Is Heaven for Everyone?

———

This is a book about heaven, written primarily for those with a Christian faith. I have tried hard to reflect what the Christian Bible has to say, rather than sharing my own hopes, thoughts and aspirations, so I must attempt to answer this question in the same spirit.

Recently, one of my friends was invited to a Royal Wedding in the UK. As you can imagine, he and his wife spent time choosing appropriate new clothes and regularly checking the invitation card. They planned the day carefully, choosing to stay in the location (Windsor) the night before, and were ready to present themselves in good time. Of course, because of all the security, they had to ensure they were dressed appropriately and, most importantly, had their invitation ready to be inspected for pre-service screening.

This was not a chore for them – it was a joy. This day was not about them, it was about the royal couple. Their privilege was to be invited and to take part. They could not and would not even think about setting their own entry criteria. They could choose not to attend. They could try and attend without the invitation card on their person. But they would only ever gain access to the wedding by following the instructions issued with the invitation.

Imagine if they turned up without the invitation and tried to blag it: 'We're related to so and so,' or, 'We're invited because of all the acts of kindness we do in the community.' You and I know that's not going to get them anywhere.

It's a little bit like that with heaven. Jesus himself used a wedding story to describe someone who tried to get into heaven without the proper clothing, issued free with the invitation, and that person was given short shrift. He never made it.[1]

Heaven, as we have seen, is not primarily about us – it's God's home and he gets to choose who gets in. Heaven is a place with no sin and with no selfishness, so on the basis of that definition alone none of us have a right to entry and none of us would ever stand a chance. Thankfully, God's desire is for everyone to make it. That's where the story of Jesus comes in.

The story of Jesus is not a story of a good man, doing good things and saying good things. The story of Jesus is the story of a sinless person dying on a cross in order that the sin and selfishness in me and in you could be forgiven, wiped clean. And so if we follow Jesus and believe in him, we are granted access, our invitation card, to heaven.

The most famous Bible verse in the world, spoken from the lips of Jesus, puts it another way: 'For God so loved the world, that he gave his only Son, that whoever believes in him should not perish but have eternal life'.[2] That's Good News!

The invitation card cannot be earned, it doesn't depend upon how many good things I've done. Bad things I have thought or done don't disqualify me. It doesn't depend on socioeconomic standing, upbringing or our family connections. Simple trust in Jesus, belief in Jesus and following him is the way in – the only way in.

If you are not certain whether you are a follower of Jesus, or if you would like to know more about what it means to become an authentic follower of Jesus and be certain of your invitation to heaven, you can email the address below and a member of our team will offer to send you some free helpful literature or put you in contact with some authentic Christians living near you.

davido@insight-marketing.com

Alternatively, you can visit https://alpha.org and discover a helpful course being run somewhere near you that has already helped tens of thousands of people find faith.

APPENDIX II

Scriptures About the Throne

——•——

Isaiah 6:1–8

Isaiah's Vision of the Lord

In the year that King Uzziah died I saw the Lord sitting upon a throne, high and lifted up; and the train of his robe filled the temple. Above him stood the seraphim. Each had six wings: with two he covered his face, and with two he covered his feet, and with two he flew. And one called to another and said:

> 'Holy, holy, holy is the LORD of hosts;
> the whole earth is full of his glory!'

And the foundations of the thresholds shook at the voice of him who called, and the house was filled with smoke. And I said: 'Woe is me! For I am lost; for I am a man of unclean lips, and I dwell in the midst of a people of unclean lips; for my eyes have seen the King, the LORD of hosts!'

Then one of the seraphim flew to me, having in his hand a burning coal that he had taken with tongs from the altar. And he touched my mouth and said: 'Behold, this has touched your lips; your guilt is taken away, and your sin atoned for.'

And I heard the voice of the Lord saying, 'Who shall I send, and who will go for us?' Then I said, 'Here am I! Send me.'

Ezekiel 1:12–28

Wherever the spirit would go, they went, without turning as they went. As for the likeness of the living creatures, their appearance was like burning coals of fire, like the appearance of torches moving to and fro among the living creatures. And the fire was bright, and out of the fire went forth lightning. And the living creatures darted to and fro, like the appearance of a flash of lightning.

Now as I looked at the living creatures, I saw a wheel on the earth beside the living creatures, one for each of the four of them. As for the appearance of the wheels and their construction: their appearance was like the gleaming of beryl. And the four had the same likeness, their appearance and construction being as it were a wheel within a wheel. When they went, they went in any of their four directions without turning as they went. And their rims were tall and awesome, and the rims of all four were full of eyes all around. And when the living creatures went, the wheels went beside them; and when the living creatures rose from the earth, the wheels rose. Wherever the spirit wanted to go, they went, and the wheels rose along with them, for the spirit of the living creatures was in the wheels. When those went, these went; and when those stood, these stood; and when those rose from the earth, the wheels rose along with them, for the spirit of the living creatures was in the wheels.

Over the heads of the living creatures there was the likeness of an expanse, shining like awe-inspiring crystal, spread out above their heads. And under the expanse their wings were stretched out straight, one towards another. And each creature had two wings covering its body. And when they went, I heard the sound of their wings like the sound of many waters, like the sound of the Almighty, a sound of tumult like the sound of an army. When they stood still, they let down their wings. And there came a voice from above the expanse over their heads. When they stood still, they let down their wings.

And above the expanse over their heads there was the likeness of a throne, in appearance like sapphire; and seated above the likeness of a throne was a likeness with a human appearance. And upwards from what had the appearance of his waist I saw as it were gleaming metal, like the appearance of fire enclosed all round. And downwards from what had the appearance of his waist I saw as it were the appearance of fire, and there was brightness around him. Like the appearance of the bow that is in the cloud on the day of rain, so was the appearance of the brightness all round.

Such was the appearance of the likeness of the glory of the LORD. And when I saw it, I fell on my face, and I heard the voice of one speaking.

Daniel 7:9–10
The Ancient of Days Reigns

As I looked,

> thrones were placed,
> and the Ancient of Days took his seat;
> his clothing was white as snow,
> and the hair of his head like pure wool;
> his throne was fiery flames;
> its wheels were burning fire.
> A stream of fire issued
> and came out from before him;
> a thousand thousands served him,
> and ten thousand times ten thousand stood before him;

Psalm 103:19

> The LORD has established his throne in the heavens,
> and his kingdom rules over all.

Revelation 4:1–8

After this I looked, and behold, a door standing open in heaven! And the first voice, which I had heard speaking to me like a trumpet, said, 'Come up here, and I will show you what must take place after this.' At once I was in the Spirit, and behold, a throne stood in heaven, with one seated on the throne. And he who sat there had the appearance of jasper and carnelian, and around the throne was a rainbow that had the appearance of an emerald. Around the throne were twenty-four thrones, and seated on the thrones were twenty-four elders, clothed in white garments, with golden crowns on their heads. From the throne came flashes of lightning, and rumblings and peals of thunder, and before the throne were burning seven torches of fire, which are the seven spirits of God, and before the throne there was as it were a sea of glass, like crystal.

And around the throne, on each side of the throne, are four living creatures, full of eyes in front and behind: the first living creature like a lion, the second living creature like an ox, the third living creature with the face of a man, and the fourth living creature like an eagle in flight. And the four living creatures, each of them with six wings, are full of eyes all around and within, and day and night they never cease to say,

'Holy, holy, holy, is the Lord God Almighty,
who was and is and is to come!'

APPENDIX III

Definitions of Heaven

When it comes to the use of the words 'heaven' and 'heavens' in scripture, and in various traditional views, we encounter a small challenge.

Several words in the Bible are translated 'heaven', but the most important ones are the Hebrew šāmayim and the Greek *ouranos*. The former is plural, and the latter often occurs in the plural. But there does not seem to be any great difference between 'heaven' and 'the heavens'. There is another Hebrew word *raqia*, translated in some places as 'firmament' or 'expanse', which seems to indicate a separating layer from sky and outer space or separating the waters above from the waters below. But this unique word is used in Ezekiel 1:22–23 in a different way to describe a layer on which God's throne sat above the chariot. We get a glimpse of writers with limited knowledge, grappling to describe what they had seen, but certainly describing some kind of almost transparent separating layer.

To make it easy for us in our English versions, the translators mostly use the plural 'heavens' when referring to the sky. An example would be Genesis 8:2, where we are told 'the heavens' were closed. When referring to the place where God dwells and where his throne is located, it's usually in the singular. An example of this would be Psalm 11:4: 'The LORD's throne is in heaven'.

We like that; it works rather easily and conveniently for us. But in the Hebrew, this binary distinction is not made. The Hebrew word is always plural, no matter what is being referred to. So, while we like a clean and clear distinction between heaven as God's address, and the heavens as sky, the original language of scripture doesn't really do this. Theologians have given several reasons why this might be, and the two most popular notions seem to be:

1. The Hebrew view of creation and the universe is a unified view and not as easily segmented as the way we tend to view the same things. In Genesis 1:1 we are told, 'God created the heavens and the earth', and from the very first descriptions available we get this sense of the sky (and probably the atmosphere), together with the invisible but 'close by' location of God. And like the clues from a treasure hunt, we get the earliest of clues that heaven and earth in God's mind, in God's purpose and in God's heart are close, and part of one created effort. It seems that the Bible views heaven, the heavens and the earth as one integrated world or one universe.

2. Some suggest that the use of the plural in Hebrew seems to be a way of expressing vastness or scale. So that, in

fact, it is the sheer size of heaven that gives rise to the plural use of the word, not the suggestion of levels.

Are There Levels of Heaven?

Interestingly, in 2 Corinthians 12:2 Paul uses the phrase 'third heaven' to describe his NDE, his trip to paradise. Most Christian scholars argue that he is simply describing God's address, as distinct from the sky and the atmosphere. It is faintly possible, that to help his readers locate his experience, he was leaning on a Jewish tradition developed more fully later in the first century AD which had seven levels of heaven; and in that Rabbinic model, paradise was allocated level 3. The full details of the seven levels each with different allocated angels and archangels can be accessed by a simple Wikipedia search,[1] and they are supported by some apocryphal material.[2]

However, interpreting purely from the canon of scripture there are only three levels of heaven, which broadly indicate the sky, the atmosphere and paradise (present heaven).

What Does the Greek Lexicon say?

Lexicon Greek 3772[3]

3772 ouranos {oo-ran-os'}

perhaps from the same as 3735 (through the idea of elevation); the sky; TDNT – 5:497,736; n m

AV – heaven 268, air 10, sky 5, heavenly + 1537; 284

1. the vaulted expanse of the sky with all things visible in it
   1a. the universe, the world
   1b. the aerial heavens or sky, the region where the clouds and the tempests gather, and where thunder and lightning are produced
   1c. the sidereal or starry heavens
2. the region above the sidereal heavens, the seat of order of things eternal and consummately perfect where God dwells and other heavenly beings

Bibliography & Works Consulted

Easy Reads

Alcorn, Randy, *Heaven* (Carol Stream, IL: Tyndale, 2004)

Burke, John, *Imagine Heaven* (Grand Rapids, MI: Baker Books, 2015)

Castle, Fiona, *Rainbows Through The Rain – An Anthology of Hope* (London: Hodder & Stoughton, 1998)

Chandler, Lauren, *Goodbye to Goodbyes: A True Story About Jesus, Lazarus and an Empty Tomb* (Epsom, UK: Good Book Company, 2019). This is a book for younger children.

Lutzer, Erwin, *One Minute After You Die* (Chicago, IL: Moody Press, 1997)

MacArthur, John, *Safe in the Arms of God: Truth from Heaven About the Death of a Child* (Nashville, TN: Thomas Nelson, 2003)

Wigglesworth, Smith, *Smith Wigglesworth on Heaven: God's Great Plan for Your Life* (New Kensington, PA: Whitaker House, 2003)

Deeper Dives

Lewis, C.S., *A Grief Observed* (London: Faber & Faber, 2013)

Gooder, Paula, *Heaven* (London: SPCK, 2011)

Gooder, Paula, *Where on Earth is Heaven?* (London: SPCK, 2015)

McGrath, Alister E., *A Brief History of Heaven* (Oxford, UK: Blackwell, 2003)

Zaleski, Carol & Philip, *The Book of Heaven* (Oxford: Oxford University Press, 2000)

References

All scripture taken from ESV unless stated otherwise

Introduction
1. 1 Corinthians 2:9, NLT

Chapter 1
1. http://www.ecology.com/birth-death-rates/ (accessed 15th June 2019)
2. Hebrews 9:27
3. http://www.ecology.com/birth-death-rates/ (accessed 15th June 2019)
4. www.notablequotes.com (accessed 15th June 2019)
5. Paul Lee Tan, *Encyclopedia of 7700 Illustrations: A Treasury of Illustrations, Anecdotes, Facts and Quotations for Pastors, Teachers and Christian Workers* (Garland TX: Bible Communications, 1979)
6. Ecclesiastes 12:7, NIV
7. Luke 23:43
8. Charles Henry Brent, https://www.goodreads.com/quotes/1011317 (accessed 4th August 2019)

9. *The Lord of the Rings: The Return of the King* (film directed by Peter Jackson, screenplay by Fran Walsh, 2003, adapted from the book by J.R.R. Tolkien)

10. Isaiah 38:10–12

11. 2 Corinthians 5:1

12. 2 Timothy 4:6

13. Philippians 1:23

14. H.C.G. Moule, *The Second Epistle to Timothy: Short Devotional Studies on the Dying Letter of St Paul – A Devotional Commentary* (Religious Tract Society, 1905)

15. Luke 16:19–31

16. Acts 7:56–60

17. Luke 8:52–55

18. 2 Corinthians 5:6,8, NIV

19. Philippians 1:21–24, NIV

Chapter 2

1. Geoffrey Parrinder, *What World Religions Teach* (London: Harrap, 1968).

2. Ecclesiastes 3:11

3. Gary Habermas, *Beyond Death* (Eugene, OR: Wipf and Stock, 2004)

4. Maurice Rawlings, *Beyond Death's Door* (New York City: Bantam Doubleday Dell, 1997)

5. Aristides, *Apology*, 15

6. Saint Cyprian, *On the Mortality*

7.   Colleen McDannell and Bernard Lang, *Heaven: A History*, 2nd edition (New Haven, CT: Yale University Press, 2001)

Chapter 3

1.   Isaac Asimov https://www.goodreads.com/quotes/347438 (accessed 5th August 2019)
2.   Sung Worship: 'a hymn' Mark 14:26; 'a hymn' 1 Corinthians 14:26
3.   David Murrow, *Why Men Hate Going to Church* (Nashville, TN: Thomas Nelson, 2011), p.87
4.   Matthew 4:8–9
5.   Jeremy Weber, 'Why Americans Go to Church or Stay Home', *Christianity Today*, August 2018. https://www.christianitytoday.com/news/2018/july/church-attendance-top-reasons-go-or-stay-home-pew.html (accessed June 2019)
6.   Jennifer LeClaire, 'When Going to Church Feels Like a Dreaded Chore', *Charisma Magazine*. https://www.charismamag.com/blogs/the-plumb-line/19451-when-going-to-church-feels-like-a-dreaded-chore (accessed June 2019)
7.   British Religion in Numbers http://www.brin.ac.uk/figures/church-attendance-in-britain-1980-2015/ (accessed June 2019)
8.   1 Peter 2:11
9.   Hebrews 11:13–16
10. 1 Peter 1:3–6

11. 2 Corinthians 5:6
12. 2nd Chapter of Acts, 'Goin' Home' from the album *With Footnotes* (Myrrh Records, 1974)
13. Charles H. Spurgeon *Morning & Evening*, April 25th morning reading (Peabody, MA: Hendrickson, 2016)
14. Ola Elizabeth Winslow, *Jonathan Edwards: Basic Writings* (New York: New American Library, 1996) p.142
15. G.K. Chesterton, *Orthodoxy* (Chicago, IL: Thomas More Association, 1985), pp.99–100
16. C.S. Lewis, *Mere Christianity*, 50th Anniversary edition (New York: HarperCollins, 2011)
17. See Hebrews 11:13–14
18. John 14:28; 17:11,24
19. Mary Reeves Davis, 'This World is Not My Home' © Sony/ATV Music Publishing LLC
20. Randy Alcorn, *Heaven* (Carol Stream, IL: Tyndale, 2004), pp.458–9

Chapter 4

1. 'Tears in Heaven' © Warner/Chappell Music, Inc, Universal Music Publishing Group
2. Psalm 57:9–11
3. Psalm 57:2–3
4. Deuteronomy 10:14
5. Genesis 1:1
6. Genesis 3:24
7. Genesis 28:17
8. 1 Peter 1:12

9. Acts 7:56
10. Acts 22:6; 26:13
11. Revelation 14:13
12. John 1:51
13. John 6:38
14. John 1:51
15. Acts 1:11
16. Acts 7:56
17. Matthew 6:9–10
18. Deuteronomy 26:15
19. Psalm 136:26; Genesis 14:22; Daniel 5:23; Matthew 5:48; Matthew 6:9
20. Nehemiah 9:6
21. Mark 13:32
22. 1 Peter 1:4
23. Acts 7:56; Hebrews 8:1
24. Revelation 4:1–2

Chapter 5

1. Revelation 21:3
2. Randy Alcorn, *Heaven* (Carol Stream, IL: Tyndale, 2004), p. 126–7
3. Colossians 1:18–20 (*MSG*)
4. Paula Gooder, *Heaven* (London: SPCK, 2011)
5. N.T. Wright *Surprised by Hope* (London: SPCK, 2007), pp. 160–4
6. Luke 23:43
7. 2 Corinthians 12:3

8. Revelation 2:7
9. Alister E. McGrath, *A Brief History of Heaven* (Oxford, UK: Blackwell, 2003), p.40
10. Fiona Castle, *Rainbows Through the Rain – An Anthology of Hope* (London: Hodder & Stoughton, 1998), p.52
11. John 14:1–2

Chapter 6

1. 2 Kings 6:17
2. 2 Corinthians 12:2–9
3. Daniel 7:9
4. Daniel 10:5–6
5. 2 Corinthians 12:7
6. 1 Corinthians 15:49
7. 1 Corinthians 15:37
8. 2 Samuel 12:23
9. 1 Samuel 28:15
10. Luke 9:30–31
11. 1 Corinthians 15:43
12. Revelation 3:4–5
13. 1 John 3:2
14. 1 Corinthians 15:49
15. 1 Corinthians 13:12
16. Revelation 2:7
17. Genesis 18:8
18. Isaiah 25:6
19. Revelation 21:1,4,22,23,27; 22:5; 19:9; 14:13
20. Revelation 7:15; 22:12; Matthew 5:12; 2 Peter 3:13;

21. Psalm 16:11
22. Ephesians 3:14
23. Revelation 14:2
24. Revelation 19:6
25. Revelation 6:9–11
26. John 14:2
27. Luke 16:19–31
28. See Steve Saint, 'Did They Have to Die?' *Christianity Today* 1996 and http://christianitymiracles.blogspot.com/2013/05/operation-auca-miracle-of-five-martyred.html (accessed July 2019)
29. Psalm 37:4
30. 1 Corinthians 2:9, NIV

Chapter 7

1. John Bunyan, *Pilgrim's Progress* (Oxford: OUP, 2003)
2. Jeremiah 23:28
3. John Burke, *Imagine Heaven* (Grand Rapids, MI: Baker Books, 2015), p.16
4. J. Steve Miller, 'Index to NDE Periodical Literature' (Durham, NC: IANDS) http://iands.org/research/index-to-nde-periodical-literature.html (Accessed June 2019)
5. van Lommel, et al, 'Near Death Experience in Survivors of Cardiac Arrest', *The Lancet*, 15 December 2001
6. Ian McCormack's story: https://www.youtube.com/watch?v=cx8QiklCcWk
7. Dale Black and Ken Gire, *Flight to Heaven* (Minneapolis, MI: Bethany House, 2010), pp. 29, 98–106

8.   Ian McCormack and Jenny Sharkey, *A Glimpse of Eternity* (New Zealand: Arun Books, 2008).

Chapter 8

1.   Matthew 6:9–10
2.   John 5:17, NIV
3.   Isaiah 9:7
4.   Isaiah 9:7–8
5.   Isaiah 6:1
6.   Ezekiel 1:26
7.   Daniel 7:9–10
8.   Psalm 103:19
9.   Revelation 4:1–2
10. Acts 7:49
11. Hebrews 12:1
12. https://quotes.thefamouspeople.com/marian-wright-edelman-2254.php (accessed July 2019)
13. Daniel 7:18
14. James Strong, *The New Strong's Exhaustive Concordance of the Bible* (Nashville, TN: Thomas Nelson, 2010) 8120 & 8121
15. Hebrews 4:1–11
16. Revelation 14:13
17. Colossians 3:23–24, NIV
18. Edward Donnelly, *Biblical Teaching on the Doctrines of Heaven and Hell* (Edinburgh: Banner of Truth, 2001)
19. Victor Hugo, http://greatthoughtstreasury.com/victor-hugo/quote/i-feel-within-me-future-life-i-am-forest-

has-been-razed-new-shoots-are-stronger-an (accessed August 2019)

20. 2 Timothy 2:12; 1 Corinthians 6:3; Luke 19:17; Revelation 2:26
21. David Gregg, *The Heaven-Life or Stimulus for Two Worlds* (Lebanon, NJ: Franklin Classics, 2018)
22. Revelation 22:3–4
23. Erwin Lutzer, *One Minute After You Die* (Chicago, IL: Moody Press, 1997), p.67

Chapter 9

1. Genesis 16
2. Genesis 21:8–19
3. Genesis 19
4. Genesis 22
5. Genesis 24
6. Genesis 28:10–17
7. Genesis 32:22–32
8. Exodus 14:19
9. Judges 6
10. Judges 13:19–20
11. Daniel 8:15–17; 10
12. Luke 1:5–20, 26–38
13. Matthew 1:19–21
14. Matthew 2
15. Matthew 4:11
16. Matthew 13:39
17. Matthew 24:30-31

18. John 1:51
19. Luke 16:22
20. Matthew 18:10
21. Matthew 22:30
22. Luke 20:36
23. Matthew 28:2
24. John 20:12
25. Acts 1:10–11
26. Acts 12:6–8
27. Acts 8:26–40
28. Acts 10
29. Acts 12:23
30. Acts 27:22–24
31. 1 Peter 3:22
32. Revelation 1:20
33. Revelation 5:2
34. Revelation 8:3
35. Revelation 8ff
36. Matthew 18:10
37. Revelation 19:10
38. Revelation 5:13
39. 1 Corinthians 13:1

Chapter 10
1. 2 Corinthians 5:10, NIV
2. Luke 10:20
3. Isaiah 62:11, NIV
4. Matthew 16:27, NIV

5. 1 Corinthians
6. Luke 18:22–30
7. Matthew 6:20–21
8. Luke 19:17
9. Luke 16:9–13
10. Proverbs 19:17
11. https://www.goodreads.com/author/quotes/2125255. Jim_Elliot (Accessed July 2019)
12. James 1:12
13. Matthew 5:11–12
14. 2 Timothy 2:12
15. Revelation 2:10; 3:11
16. Matthew 25:21–23; Luke 19:17
17. See Matthew 6:33; Hebrews 11:6
18. 1 Thessalonians 2:19, NIV
19. 1 Peter 5:2–4
20. Colossians 3:23–24; 4:1

Chapter 11

1. Revelation 2:7
2. Revelation 21
3. 22:1–5
4. 2 Peter 3:8–13
5. 1 Corinthians 15:51–52
6. 1 Thessalonians 4:13 – 5:1
7. Hebrews 1:11-12
8. 1 Corinthians 15:42–44

Chapter 12

1. 1 Corinthians 15:54–57
2. Matthew 5:4
3. 1 Corinthians 15:50
4. Erwin Lutzer, *One Minute After You Die* (Chicago, IL: Moody Press, 1997) pp.77–9
5. Song based on Psalm 63:3–4 by Hugh Mitchell, 'Thy Loving Kindness' ©1956 New Spring (Admin. by Brentwood-Benson Music Publishing, Inc.)
6. Psalm 63:3, NASB
7. Matthew 5:4
8. Psalm 23:4
9. If you would like to listen to the family tributes broadcast for Joel Oliver visit: http://bit.ly/DavidTribute or http://bit.ly/Familytribute
10. Psalm 116:15–16, NIV
11. Revelation 1:18, NIV
12. Hebrews 9:27
13. Erwin Lutzer, *One Minute After You Die* (Chicago, IL: Moody Press, 1997) pp.123–4
14. Quoted in Lee Strobel, *The Case for Faith: A Journalist Investigates the Toughest Objections to Christianity* (Grand Rapids, MI: Zondervan, 2000) p.47
15. Ecclesiastes 8:8

Chapter 13

1. John 11:33–36
2. Acts 8:2

3. Philippians 2:27, NIV
4. Isaiah 61:1
5. Psalm 34:18
6. Spoken in January 2019 by Dr Eleanor Fulton
7. Psalm 56:8
8. Anne Doughty, *A Girl Called Rosie*, The Hamiltons Series, Book 4 (London: Allison & Busby, 2008)
9. Anne Doughty, *Shadow on the Land*, The Hamiltons Series, Book 6 (London: Allison & Busby, 2010) pp.111–12
10. Alfred Lord Tennyson, 'Break, Break, Break', 1842
11. Henry Alford, 'Ten Thousand Times Ten Thousand', 1867

Appendix I

1. Matthew 22:11–12
2. John 3:16

Appendix III

1. https://en.wikipedia.org/wiki/Heaven_in_Judaism (accessed July 2019)
2. 'The Third Book of Enoch'
3. James Strong, *The New Strong's Concise Dictionary of the Words in the Greek Testament and The Hebrew Bible* (Bellingham, WA: Faithlife, 2009)

Made in the USA
Coppell, TX
13 May 2021

55366133R00144